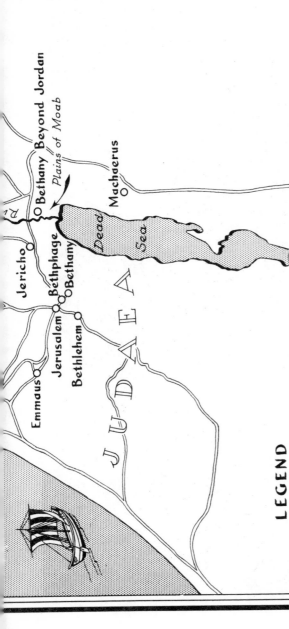

MEN
CALLED HIM
MASTER

By ELWYN ALLEN SMITH

ISBN 0-88019-210-0

Illustrated by Harold Minton

Schmul Publishing Co., Inc.
Wesleyan Book Club   1987   Salem, Ohio

Printed by
Old Paths Tract Society Inc.
Shoals, Indiana 47581

CONTENTS

Have You Ever Wondered? 6

1   A Voice in the Wilderness 7

2   Fishers of Men 14

3   A Man of Authority 25

4   God Is Now King! 34

5   Who Is This Carpenter? 45

6   The Old and the New 54

7   Missionaries of the Kingdom 64

8   He Is More than a Teacher 74

9   How Will You Know the Messiah? . . . 80

10   "You Are the Christ" 88

11   A Secret Is Told 102

12   The Greatest Among Us 113

13   The Messiah Must Die 122

14   A Day of Victory 131

15   Dispute in the Temple 141

16   The End of Hope 152

17   The Darkest Hour of All 165

18   The Rock of Faith 173

HAVE YOU EVER WONDERED?

*W*HAT *kind of men were Jesus' disciples? What was it like to be with Jesus in Palestine? Why did some of the disciples find it so hard to understand Jesus? Who were the people who killed Jesus? Why did they do it? This book has been written to help you to answer these questions. It takes you right into Jesus' world so that you can hear his conversations with the disciples and watch the things they did.*

The stories of Jesus and the disciples in this book are told in different words from those you will find in your Bible, and background has been built in from other records of the time. For example, the Bible gives only the fact that one of the disciples was a Zealot; in this book the disciple is shown speaking and acting as we know Zealots spoke and acted. The story of the rich young ruler has been placed early in Jesus' ministry to show that he would not accept every man who wanted to be his disciple. The parable of the Good Samaritan has also been placed in the early period as an example of the informal way in which Jesus taught. That you may know what is from the Bible and what is added to make a complete story, Scripture references for each event are given in the back of the book. These references will help you to read and understand the Gospels. As you read what it meant to be a disciple of Jesus while he was on earth, you will see more clearly what it means to be one of his disciples today.

1. A VOICE IN THE WILDERNESS

ANDREW! The baskets are slipping!" Two men on foot were driving heavily loaded donkeys ahead of them. Across the back of Andrew's tiny beast hung two huge baskets. One slanted crazily forward.

"It ought to hold until we get to the top," answered Andrew. He looked critically at the load and then at the path ahead. They were climbing the bank of a wide gully cut by the floods that rushed down from the barren hills into the valley of the Jordan River every spring. Andrew shouted a command and the donkeys climbed slowly upward. At the top the men stopped to catch their breath.

"John," exclaimed Andrew in disgust, "I have tightened this thing on every hill between Galilee and Judea!" He worked impatiently at the knotted ropes that bound the baskets on the donkey's back. John was not listening. He was gazing at the scene before them.

Torrents of muddy water poured through the gully during the season of rains. Now the clay in the bottom was dry and cracked. Under the hoofs of the animals it was as hard as stone. John pushed his damp hair back from his forehead. His home province, with its green hillsides surrounding the cool Lake of Galilee, was very different from this burnt, rocky land of Judea, which lay southwest of where they stood. The gully carried a sluggish stream of heated air up from the valley; he could feel the damp warmth on his skin. Even on the hilltop there was no cooling breeze.

Andrew wiped his face with a dusty sleeve and left a dirty streak above his brows. "There!" he exclaimed. "These baskets ought to stay on now." The rope was drawn tightly around the belly of the donkey.

"We should be at Bethany soon," remarked John.

Andrew struck the donkey with his whip and said gruffly, "Come on!" as though the animal had shaken its load loose on purpose. The little caravan started again, Andrew in the lead.

The road was built on the slope of the hills which closed in the plain of the Jordan. Stretching far to the west the men could see fields of ripe grain. The heat of early summer had come quickly this year and now threatened to destroy the crop. Farmers were hard at work cutting the wheat and threshing out the grain on platforms of earth pressed smooth as stone.

"Are you sure that John the Baptizer is still at Bethany?" called Andrew over his shoulder. John did not answer. After a moment, Andrew added, "Perhaps he has gone to some other place to preach." Still there was no reply. Irritated, Andrew turned. John had dropped behind and was walking with a stranger. Where had this traveler come from? He must have been moving fast to overtake them so swiftly. His robe was hitched high at the waist for easier walking. Andrew slowed and waited for the men.

"Could you tell us, friend, where John the Prophet is baptizing?" John was saying.

The traveler smiled. "I hear he is at Bethany on the Jordan, near Jericho. Do you want to hear him?"

"We are his disciples," responded John proudly; then he bit his lip. Andrew was frowning at him. It was dangerous to say a thing like that! John looked at the stranger narrowly. He was from Galilee; his broad accent showed that. John glanced at Andrew. Surely a Galilean was safe! "The Prophet says that Israel will soon be free," ventured John. It was a test question. The stranger smiled as though he agreed, and Andrew asked enthusiastically: "Do you believe him? He says that God will overthrow the Romans soon!"

"How does John the Baptizer think all this will happen?" asked the Galilean traveler. Andrew did not reply for a long while. Finally he said: "The Prophet tells us that we cannot set ourselves free without God's help. He says that if we had been willing to change our ways, God would have rescued us long ago. Therefore we must get rid of sin and pride and take our stand on God's side. When we do that, great things will happen!" He looked directly at his fellow traveler. "Do you believe this?"

The stranger's answer was clear. "John speaks the truth."

Suddenly they heard the thunder of galloping hoofs. A band of horsemen was bearing down on them. Helmets and spears glinted in the brilliant sunlight. Andrew and John shouted at the donkeys, but one of them moved slowly. Desperately John whipped the animal. The donkey leaped. A rope snapped and one of the heavy baskets dropped to the ground.

The three men heard a soldier curse them. They could hardly see each other for the thick dust. The basket lay trampled in the dirt; salted fish were scattered all over the road. Andrew kicked the ruined basket into the ditch. "May God soon burn Rome and all her soldiers! This land belongs to us!" He ran a few steps as if to overtake the riders and shook his fist. "God will strike you!" he shouted. The stranger was helping John put what was left of the fish in the other three baskets. Andrew turned to them.

"I have seen whole armies of Romans march through fields of ripe wheat! I have seen our towns burned by these destroyers!

They have killed thousands of our people! We have seen even our own friends killed by these murderers!"

The man answered quietly: "I know what they have done. But hating them will not help." Andrew was taken by surprise.

"We have been oppressed before," continued the stranger. "God has sent John to us now, just as he has always sent prophets to tell us what we should do."

"What should we do?"

"Just as you said yourself, we must repent of our sin," replied the traveler. "God can do very little until he finds men who are willing to obey him." Andrew had nothing to say.

"There is a well not far ahead," remarked John. "We must water the animals." Under a dusty palm over the next hill they found the well. The stranger drew water for the donkeys and they drank noisily. Then he drew water for the men. They had no sooner finished than Andrew urged: "Let's hurry. We are not far from the place where John is baptizing."

The road led down the slope and across the plain toward the river, which had cut a deep gorge. At the edge the men paused to look. A hundred feet below flowed the Jordan. It seemed sluggish now; but in the rainy season it was swift and treacherous. The water was yellow and gray and only a few shrubs clung to the banks. A short distance away the river turned and disappeared behind the opposite cliff.

"The crossing is below that bend," explained John to the stranger. "The Prophet should be there." He gave his donkey a cut with the whip, and the stolid animal moved faster. A few minutes later he cried out: "There! See down there?" People were gathered at the edge of the river. It did not take the men long to reach the gully through which the road descended to the river. The fishermen tied their donkeys with the other animals that stood tethered to bushes and small trees. In their haste they forgot their companion.

"Do you see the Prophet?" inquired Andrew, looking eagerly about. John jerked at his sleeve.

"There! By that rock on the bank!" They climbed up the slope where they could see.

John could not tell why he felt the way he did. It might

have been the appearance of John the Baptizer. He wore a rough camel-hair tunic and a leather belt. None of the people who were there for the first time had ever seen such a man before. He was very thin. His skin was tanned brown and his hair and beard were long. Like the poorest people in Palestine, he lived on grasshoppers and wild honey. Just then John the Baptizer spoke. He looked old, but his voice showed that he was young and strong.

"It is time you begin to show some sign that you are God's chosen people," he cried out. "But you are just like your ancestors—you pay no attention to God. You don't listen to the prophets. God is not going to wait much longer. The time has come to repent! The Kingdom of Heaven is near!"

The crowd stirred. What was this? Could it be true that the end of the world was coming soon?

"Isaiah the Prophet said, 'Everyone shall see the saving power of God,'" continued the Baptizer. "God is getting ready to clean off his threshing platform. He will gather his wheat into his storehouse, but he will burn the straw in fire that never dies down! Let every one of you get ready for the coming of the Lord!"

Near the front edge of the crowd a priest stood up. "How do you dare talk this way?" he demanded. "Who are you—the Messiah?"

"No, I am not the Messiah," replied the Prophet.

"Then who are you? The Prophet Elijah?"

"I am not Elijah."

"Are you Moses come back to us?"

"No."

"Then who are you? The rulers in Jerusalem have sent me to find out. What have you to say for yourself?" Andrew and John glanced at each other. The rulers!

John the Baptizer called out boldly to the whole crowd, "I am a voice crying in the wilderness, 'Clear the way for the Lord!'"

The priest from Jerusalem interrupted again. "If you are not the Christ, nor Elijah, nor Moses, what right have you to baptize people?" The people stirred; they did not like this man.

"I baptize you with water for repentance, but he who is coming after me is mightier. I am not fit even to tie his sandal laces. He will baptize you with the Holy Spirit and fire. You must repent!"

A man broke away from the crowd and stepped uncertainly toward the Prophet. Words came from his lips as though it hurt him to speak. "I have forced money out of people. I am a tax-gatherer. What can I do?" Everyone there had been cheated by tax collectors.

"Turn your whole life back toward God. Never again force people to pay more money than is just."

Several other people had joined the tax collector. "What must I do?" asked a soldier.

"Never take money from people by force. Never blackmail. Be content with your pay." He looked at the group before him and said: "Let every man of you who owns two garments share with the person who has none at all. If you have food, share it too!"

A whisper ran over the crowd. John had turned to some religious officials, Sadducees and Pharisees, who stood watching. "You nest of snakes! Who told you to flee from God's day of judgment? It is time you repented!"

"How can he talk that way to Pharisees?" said Andrew. He could tell even from where he stood that the Pharisees felt the charge was unjust.

"Why should we repent?" asked one of them. "We are descended from Abraham himself. We were born to be God's chosen people!"

"God can make children of Abraham out of these rocks if he wants!" burst out the Prophet. "Instead of saying over and over again, 'Abraham is our ancestor,' you ought to live so that people will know that you have repented! The wood chopper is ready to destroy every tree that is not producing good fruit. Every bad tree he will cut down and throw into the fire!" John turned his back on them.

"Look!" whispered Andrew in excitement. "There is the stranger we met on the road!"

The Prophet had walked down into the water to begin baptizing those who were waiting on the shore, but now he stopped and turned toward the place where the Galilean was standing. He completely forgot the crowd. In the silence Andrew could hear him protesting.

"No! No! No!" The Prophet stepped back in awe. "I am not worthy to baptize you. You should baptize me!" The two fishermen could not hear the Galilean's reply, but they saw him walk down into the water, John the Baptizer leading. The people stood as though fascinated. Recalling the incident later on, Andrew and John realized that their tense concentration on the two men at the river had driven every other thought from their minds.

John was baptizing the stranger. As he came up from the river, the Galilean's face bore an expression of joy and praise which the fishermen remembered as long as they lived. Some power had come upon him.

"What happened, Andrew? What happened?"

Andrew did not hear; he was staring at the Galilean.

"Andrew!" John was insistent. "Something just happened. I don't understand. What was it?"

Andrew murmured. "He must be a prophet too."

The people were talking excitedly. Everyone felt as John and Andrew did. The Galilean had gone, and the Prophet was now baptizing the others who waited. Shadows were creeping into the gorge as evening approached. Groups started away toward the near-by towns.

"Did you hear what the Galilean said to John the Baptizer?" asked John. Without answering, Andrew started toward the knot of people near the Prophet, and John followed. Andrew asked a man beside him, "Did you hear what the Galilean said to the Prophet?"

"Yes," the man answered. "He said, 'Every man must take his stand on God's side.' " Before Andrew could say any more the Prophet spoke. He knew what the people were thinking.

"Upon the head of this man of Galilee I saw the Spirit of God settle like a dove from the sky," he declared. "God has chosen him to do His work!"

2. FISHERS OF MEN

THE morning sun was breaking over the hills that closed in the Lake of Galilee on the east. Fog was thick over the water, but the fishermen in the two boats that lay a short distance from the shore knew the sun had risen, for the mist was full of white light. Between the boats was a great net, partly under water. The fishermen, two in each boat, were pulling the opposite edges over the side into the bottom of their boats. Their breath hung in the chilly air. Andrew had returned to Galilee after his trip to Judea and was working with his brother, Simon.

"I wouldn't mind hard work if we could catch fish," remarked Simon, resting a moment.

"We'll soon see what we've caught," replied Andrew. The net was almost gathered in.

"It won't be much," grunted Simon, bending to his work again. After a few minutes the boats lay side by side, the nets heaped high in them.

"I have fished in this lake all my life," remarked James, the brother of John, "and so has my father, Zebedee, but I have never seen so few fish for a night's work!"

Andrew felt as disgusted as Simon and James, but all he said was, "Let's go ashore."

James and Andrew guided the boats toward the spot where Zebedee had built a fire of thorn twigs. The men jumped out and crowded around the crackling flames. Zebedee had chosen several fish for their breakfast. He raked some hot coals from the fire and laid the fish among them. They smelled good to the hungry men. This was the best time of the fishermen's day. Hard work was done. The fire was warm. The thought of food gave them a good feeling.

"Father, why is fishing so poor this year?" asked John.

"I don't know, son," replied Zebedee. "Some years there are enough fish for all Galilee and Judea. But in years like this, the people of the five cities on our lake go hungry." He was thinking of times past. "If the wheat crop is poor in Galilee, there may be riots."

"That would only make matters worse," commented Simon.

"Yes, unless King Herod has improved lately." Zebedee smiled sourly. "I think that foreigner actually enjoys killing. How he loves our money! If riots come, we are sure to be taxed even more." He took two of the fish off the coals and laid them on a smooth rock. When they were cool enough, he picked them up. "Breakfast is ready," he said. The men rose and bowed their heads, while the older man prayed.

"Praise ye the Lord.
I will give thanks unto the Lord with my whole heart,
In the council of the upright, and in the congregation.
He hath given food unto them that fear him:
He will ever be mindful of his promise.
Holy and reverend is his name. Amen."

While they ate, James asked, "Father, who is in the other boat this morning?" Zebedee hired men to work for him.

"Old Gideon the farmer, with our new man, a gentile from Sidon."

"Why in the world did you hire a gentile, father?" asked John sharply.

"Well, son, he is young and strong. He is willing to work for us." He paused. "But I couldn't help wondering where he came from."

"Did you ask him?"

"No. He wouldn't answer questions about himself. But he knew fishing." John shook his head.

"I don't like it, father. Jews have no business working with gentiles. And besides, if he is a runaway slave, we might get into trouble."

"Now look, son. Half the people in Galilee are gentiles. Every day we see them. What harm is there in working with them?"

"Here comes the other boat," said Simon. The sun was driving away the mist; Simon pointed to a fishing boat drawing closer to the shore.

"Did you do any better than we did, Gideon?" called Zebedee. As the old farmer came toward them, the men could tell that his body was rugged in spite of stooped shoulders. "No better; maybe worse. It's getting as hard to make a living on the lake as by plowing the land."

The newcomers sat down and hungrily ate the fish that Simon handed them.

"Zebedee says there may be riots if the wheat is poor," said Simon. "What do you think of the crop, Gideon?"

Gideon squinted toward the hills as though looking at the fields that lay beyond them. "My guess is that there will be enough." He frowned. "Enough, that is, if the landlords don't grab it all."

James glanced at Simon, concealing a smile. Old Gideon never got tired of scolding the big landowners.

"Before I was forced off my farm, we had plenty to eat, even in dry weather." He shook his finger. "And mind you, I had only five acres! Now look what has happened!" He pounded his knee. "A man can hardly feed his family with ten acres. Why? Taxes and more taxes!" He counted on his fingers. "First, Herod takes one fourth of all our grain. That goes into the bellies of the Romans. Then there is the tithe. That takes enough to feed a hired man! Then we pay the Temple tax to feed the priests. They get the first-born of all the sheep too. When a man's first son is born, he must make a big gift to the synagogue. Farmers have to give part of the wool at sheep-shearing; part of the wood at woodcutting; and the best of the fruit at harvest." He looked around and spat on the ground. "On top of that we pay for the schools and synagogues! Is it any wonder we have hardly enough left to feed ourselves?"

"But religious taxes are paid for the sake of God, Gideon!" protested James.

"Yes, yes . . . I know." Gideon couldn't argue the point; for a moment he was silent. Then he looked sharply at James and snapped: "Do the landlords pay religious taxes? No!" His voice was bitter. "That taxgatherer who bought me out knew ways to get out of paying the Temple tax!"

"Was it when you sold your farm that you became a fisherman, Gideon?" asked James.

"Yes. I almost had to serve a term of bondage."

The gentile jerked up his head and said, "Were you a slave?"

"No, but my brother bound himself for twelve years," answered Gideon, looking at the gentile curiously.

"Do the bondslaves make much trouble here?" he asked.

Zebedee looked at him very closely. "In Galilee the slaves do not cause riots. The Jews do."

James explained. "In Palestine there are more free men than slaves. Hunger causes most riots. But in a way, our whole nation is a slave to Rome." His eyes challenged the gentile and no one missed his meaning when he spoke again. "A nation can't run away from its master the way a slave can."

The gentile started. He glanced swiftly around the group. The men were looking at him suspiciously.

"Are you a runaway slave?" demanded Zebedee point-blank.

The man flushed and spoke shamefacedly. "Yes," he admitted.

After a moment's silence, Andrew said: "The Romans treat us all the same way. No one here will betray you." The man's face showed his relief.

"Perhaps you will tell us where you are from," suggested Simon.

"I am a Greek; a fisherman from Corinth. I was taken captive and made the slave of a Roman soldier. We were sent to Sidon." He waved his hand toward the west. "I watched my chance and ran away. Here I want to work and remain unknown."

John said: "Will you come with us to the synagogue? If you are going to work with us, you should become one of us."

"I will worship any god who will give me a happy life."

"I can't promise that God will do that," answered John. "Our nation has always suffered greatly." He looked at Andrew. "But we believe what John the Baptizer tells us: God is soon coming to save us."

The gentile shook his head. "I don't understand."

"Perhaps he has not heard of the Prophet," Andrew said to Simon. He turned to the slave and said, "God has sent a Prophet to warn us to turn back to God."

"What will your god do for you?" asked the other.

Andrew spoke sternly to him. "God is not our servant! We are his servants! We obey him."

"John the Baptizer says God will soon set up his Kingdom," added John.

"I must say the Zealots make better sense to me," interrupted Simon. "After all, you have to make some effort yourself. You can't just sit and wait."

"Who are the Zealots?" asked the gentile.

"They are warlike patriots who are always staging riots against the Romans," explained Simon.

"While I was at Sidon, the Romans were busy hunting down bands of these people," observed the gentile.

"Many brave men have been killed by Rome. We seem to be defeated in every rebellion." Simon turned to his brother. "Do you remember Judah the Galilean?" Andrew nodded.

"Judah was a Zealot," continued Simon. "He gathered a

group of brave young Jews and raided one of Herod's forts. They took swords, spears, and money to buy food. At the Feast of the Passover, they came out of their hiding places in the northern hills." He pointed toward the mountains where the snowy crest of Mount Hermon shone in the morning light. "They hid swords under their robes and joined the crowds going to Jerusalem. I was only a child but my parents took me to Jerusalem that year.

"The Zealots knew the Temple would be guarded by Roman soldiers, so they surrounded it. The Roman commander saw men with swords in the crowd of pilgrims filling the Temple and thought they were going to attack his men, so he ordered his soldiers to attack first.

"The Zealots were taken by surprise and the Romans gained the upper hand. Then Judah saw his chance. He rallied his men, and they climbed on the roof of the wooden buildings which surround the Temple courtyard. From there they threw spears down on the Romans. It looked then as though they had a chance to win.

"To drive the Jews off these buildings, the Romans set them afire. They were dry as tinder and burned fiercely. The Zealots had to get down. Some killed themselves rather than surrender. Others leaped among the Romans and died fighting. Those that escaped to the country hid in the hills around Jerusalem. There Judah gathered together as many of his men as were still alive.

"The Roman general sent bands of his men into the hills to hunt down the survivors. One morning there was a blare of trumpets and a group of Roman soldiers came marching down the street. From the roof of the house where I stayed with my parents we saw Judah of Galilee being prodded along by guards in armor. He was hurt but he walked proudly.

"I began to cry. Even my father had tears in his eyes. Although I was only a young boy, I knew that Judah would be killed for fighting the Romans. But I did not know how terrible it would be.

"The Romans made all Jews who did not live in Jerusalem leave within two days. It was a sad time. We had come in joy, remembering how at the first Passover Feast God had protected us from the Egyptians. We left sorrowing. We saw a dreadful sight when we went out of the city gate."

The fishermen had finished their food and sat with their eyes fixed on Simon. James and Andrew had heard bits of this story before, but listened eagerly for details as Simon talked. John's eyes seemed to be saying: "Go on! Go on!" Zebedee was older and knew the story well. Already his face showed pain and sorrow.

"Judah had been condemned to die as a criminal. All criminals were crucified. He was thrown to the ground and his body was spread on a wooden cross. His hands were nailed to the crossbeam. His feet were nailed also. The cross was set upright beside the road from Jerusalem to Galilee. All the Zealots who had been hiding in the hills of Judea were crucified with him.

"When my father and mother took me out through the city gate, I saw hundreds of crosses on both sides of the road. On each cross hung a brave Galilean. When I saw that Judah was dead, my boyhood dream crumbled. I have never forgotten."

The fire had burned out while Simon talked. The morning sun glared on the gray ashes. Lost in thought, the men gazed at the dead fire. Finally Simon said: "It seems that every time we fight for the Kingdom of God we suffer all the more. How does John the Baptizer explain that, Andrew?"

"He didn't say anything about it that I remember," Andrew admitted.

People were hurrying along the road back of the beach.

"Come along, men," said Zebedee briskly. "We must clean the nets."

"I think I'll try my luck in the shallow water," said Andrew. He picked up a circular net with weights around the edges. He waded to his knees and threw the net. It fell flat on the water and sank, trapping a small fish under it.

The others began to wash the nets, patiently picking out the seaweed and pebbles caught in them.

"Say! What's going on?" John pointed to a knot of people following a man who was walking along the beach.

"Probably some trader," remarked Simon.

"He looks more like a teacher to me," said John.

"Why not go over and see?" suggested Simon.

In a moment John came running back. "It is Jesus, the Galilean whom Andrew and I saw with John the Baptizer! Andrew! Andrew!" he called. "Come and see him, Simon. Come on!"

"I think I had better finish cleaning this net, John."

"But this man is a Prophet!"

"You go ahead if you want to." John gave Simon a disgusted look. When he turned toward the crowd of people, he noticed that they were moving toward him.

I wish they would come over here, thought John. As if he had read John's mind, Jesus walked nearer the fisherman. Everyone was listening to a scribe who was asking questions. Scribes knew the religious laws and the sacred books thoroughly.

"How can I get into this Kingdom you are telling us about, Rabbi?"

"What is written in the Law? What do you read there?" asked Jesus. The scribe answered: "You must love the Lord your God with your whole heart, your whole soul, your whole strength, and your whole mind. Also, love your neighbor as yourself."

"Correct," said Jesus. "Do that and you will live." Simon's hands were busy, but he smiled to hear Jesus answer the educated man so easily.

The scribe felt foolish because Jesus had made him answer his own question. Hoping to escape embarrassment, he asked, "Just who is my neighbor, Master?"

"There was once a man traveling from Jerusalem to Jericho," answered Jesus. "He was attacked by some robbers who took everything he had and left him badly hurt. After a while a priest came by, but when he caught sight of the man lying in the ditch bleeding, he went on without even looking a second time. A Levite came along a little later and he too passed by on the other side of the road. Then a Samaritan came along." Simon was listening intently. Like most of the people there, he looked down on Samaritans, and wondered why Jesus had brought this one into the story.

"The two Jews had done nothing to help their fellow countryman, but the Samaritan stopped," continued Jesus. "He put salve on his wounds and tied them up. He put him on his own donkey and took him to an inn by the road. He paid his bill so that he could stay as long as it would take to get well. When the Samaritan left, he said to the manager: 'Take care of him. If you have to do more for him, I will pay you back when I come this way again.'" Jesus looked at the scribe. "Which of these three men was a true neighbor to the man who was beaten?"

"The man who was kind to him," admitted the scribe grudgingly.

"Then go and be like that yourself!" said Jesus.

Simon looked at Jesus amazed, the net in his hand completely forgotten. *Not even John the Baptizer would say the Samaritan was better than the others,* he thought to himself. *No wonder Andrew and John had talked so much about this Rabbi whom they had first met in Judea!*

Attracted by the crowd, many more people had come down from the road. They were pressing in on Jesus so much that he turned to Simon and asked abruptly, "May I use your boat?"

Simon was taken by surprise but he quickly recovered himself and said, "Certainly, Rabbi."

Jesus asked him to push out a little way. Then he turned around and spoke to the people on the shore. "The Kingdom of God does not come like a flash of lightning so that you can say, 'Here it is!' The Kingdom of God is right now in your midst."

"Does that mean that our enemies will be destroyed soon, Rabbi?" asked Simon eagerly.

"The Kingdom of God does not come by violence and bloodshed," answered Jesus, "but by the power of God. It is not his will that you should kill persons whom you hate. You should love your enemies! Do good to those who hate you! Pray for those who abuse you. If a man slaps your cheek, let him slap the other one too. If he steals your coat, give him your shirt too.

"If you love only people who love you, what does that amount to? Even bad men do that! It is your enemies that you must love and help. You must give without expecting to be paid back."

"That is impossible!" exclaimed Simon in dismay.

"God's Kingdom has power to change all kinds of men," said Jesus, looking straight at Simon. "His power is like a piece of yeast in a bowl of dough—the tiny bit of yeast quickly works its way through all the dough until every bit is changed. The Kingdom of God is also like a tiny mustard seed. It is so small that a farmer can hardly see it mixed with his wheat. But this tiny seed is so powerful that when it is planted it grows larger than most trees."

Simon shook his head. He did not say anything, but he doubted if any such power existed.

"Will you push the boat out into deep water?" asked Jesus. "I want you to lower the net for a catch of fish."

"Rabbi, we fished all night and took nothing," protested Simon. "But if you wish, I will try again." Much puzzled by this sudden request, the two fishermen pulled toward deep water. The people on the shore watched them put up the oars; the boat drifted slowly in the wind. The two men lowered the net. It had hardly sunk below the surface of the water when the fishermen knew that they had dropped it directly in the path of a great school of fish. Startled into action, they pulled desperately at the net, but it was too heavy. The cords began to break. In great excitement Andrew stood up and shouted to James, "Come and help us!"

With James and John drawing the opposite edge of the net into their boat, the four men succeeded in saving the huge catch. Jesus sat quietly watching from the back of the boat, which was now filled with fish to the point of sinking. Simon looked at Jesus and a strange fear took hold of him. There had been no fish all night—and now, at the bidding of this Rabbi, they had caught hundreds! Impulsively he fell on his knees at Jesus' feet and said: "Lord, I do need to be changed! I am a sinful man!"

"The Kingdom of Heaven is like a net that catches all kinds of fish, Simon," replied Jesus. "You must follow me. From now on you shall fish for men." From the other boat, James and John had been listening to every word that Jesus had spoken. He now turned to Andrew and the two others. "If you will follow me, you too shall become fishers of men."

When the boat came to shore, the people looked in amazement at the great haul of fish, but the catch meant nothing to the four fishermen. Without a single word they left Zebedee and followed Jesus back to Capernaum.

3. A MAN OF AUTHORITY

IT WAS not long before reports of the new Rabbi at Capernaum had traveled to all the cities around the Lake of Galilee. At Bethsaida, a little town three miles across the lake from Capernaum, farmers gossiped about the news as they worked in the green fields on the hills above their town. The name of Jesus was on the lips of everyone in the noisy market place; but the fishermen on the beaches knew most about the Teacher who said that the Kingdom of God was very near.

One Friday afternoon, a fisherman from Bethsaida, named Philip, was netting fish from his small boat at the northern tip of the Lake of Galilee. The Jordan River emptied into the lake at this point, and there were often large fish to be caught. Spawned and fattened in the many tiny streams that flowed into the upper Jordan, they came down the river to feed on the weeds that grew thickly in the swamps at the river mouth.

Philip glanced up at the sun. It was well past noon, time to be leaving. Philip drew his net into the boat, set the oars into their crude notches, and rowed steadily toward Bethsaida, about a mile distant. He would have just enough time, he reflected, to clean up, get back to the boat, and row across the lake before the Sabbath Day commenced at sunset.

Philip landed and drew his boat a short distance up on the beach.

"Say, Philip! Why don't you pull it up farther?" Philip looked around and saw a friend cleaning a net. Without pausing he replied, "I am going to use it again."

"Are you going far?" But the question was not answered; Philip was already hastening up the narrow street toward his home. An hour later, he returned. Anxiously he glanced toward the sun, now nearing the horizon.

"Where are you going?" asked the fisherman. Philip kept his back turned to the curious man. After he had launched the rowboat and was pulling away, he called out, "Across the lake." He knew the man had asked only to find out if he would be back before the Sabbath started.

Nevertheless, Philip rowed hard for Capernaum; he was conscientious and did not want to break the Sabbath if he could help it. The white walls and small domed houses of Capernaum were only a quarter of a mile away when Philip heard a sound that told him he had left Bethsaida too late.

The minister of the synagogue at Capernaum had blown his trumpet. Philip twisted around and saw that the mellow note had come just as the red sun sank behind the hills west of the lake. There were two more long blasts. From this moment, the Sabbath rest began.

The minister laid the trumpet down on the flat roof of his house. No Jew worked after this signal. The women had already brought a full day's supply of water into their houses and were forbidden to carry any more. Fishermen were not supposed to clean nets or row. The market place was silent, for no buying or selling was permitted. The minister did not even carry his trumpet into the house. He would wait until sunset on Saturday when the Sabbath ended and then he would put it away.

He lighted the great synagogue lamp. This was part of Sabbath worship and did not count as work. This shining light, hanging where Philip could plainly see it as he drew his boat up on the beach in front of Capernaum, made him feel a little guilty. Hurriedly he stored the oars under the seats and set out for the home of Simon, his friend in the city.

Simon's house was in a high part of Capernaum, set back against the hills. It was not a long walk for Philip through the streets that led up from the lake front. Leaving the street of hard-packed dirt, Philip went under an arch into a square courtyard, open to the sky. The house was built on four sides, and doors led from a narrow porch into the rooms. Philip hesitated a moment and then knocked at one of the doors.

"Philip!" Simon stood in the doorway, smiling at his friend. His broad shoulders and short neck made him seem burly. "Come in, my friend!" Simon called across the courtyard to his wife: "Bring some food! Philip has come."

Inside, oil lamps were lighted and Simon's children were playing on the floor in a corner of the room. Philip was very fond of them. He ran his fingers through the hair of the oldest, a black-haired lad of seven. The child gave him a friendly smile.

"What brings you to us on the Sabbath, Philip?" inquired Simon, half teasing, half reproving.

"I did not leave the river mouth until about three o'clock," explained Philip, a bit ashamed. "I was very eager to come to Capernaum."

Simon was immediately curious. "What made you come?"

"Everyone in Bethsaida is talking about the new Rabbi who is teaching here," answered Philip. "They say that he talks of a new kingdom." Philip was a little surprised to see how intently Simon was listening to his words, but he did not pause. "I thought you could tell me more about him. I hear that he comes from Nazareth. When did you first find out about him?"

"A couple of months ago John and Andrew went up to Jerusalem and when they came back they told us they had met this man," answered Simon. "They saw him baptized by John the Baptizer. The Prophet told them that Jesus was going to be a mighty servant of God. We didn't take it very seriously though —you know how enthusiastic Andrew gets.

"We never realized what kind of person Jesus was until we saw him ourselves," continued Simon. "He isn't like an ordinary teacher. You feel that he is so sure of himself and yet he is so humble." Simon was deeply earnest. "Everything he says goes right to your heart, Philip. I can hardly understand what it is—there is some power in him!" Simon's wife entered.

"Here is food for you," said Simon, as his wife set a bowl of boiled fish on the table. Hungry from his trip across the lake, Philip gratefully moved to the rough bench in front of the table and began to eat.

After a while he asked, "Then you know this Rabbi well?"

"Yes," answered Simon. "He has been down on the lake shore every day this week. I have been with him most of the time."

"Doesn't that take a good deal of time away from fishing?" observed Philip.

"Yes, some," replied Simon. "We do some fishing early in the mornings. But it is true that we don't do very much."

Philip was thoroughly puzzled by now. Simon had always been a hard worker. But Philip could not think of a way to ask why his friend had changed. For a while Simon remained silent. Nervously his foot stirred the palm fronds that covered the floor. "You see, Philip," he finally said very hesitantly, "I have really stopped fishing. I am now a follower of Jesus."

Philip was dumfounded. "You mean you aren't working with Andrew and James and John any more?"

"They have left Zebedee too," answered Simon.

"What in the world . . ." blurted Philip. He stopped short. "How are you going to feed your wife and children?" he asked.

Simon looked at Philip frankly. "I do not know, Philip," he said, his voice firm. "But this one thing I am sure of: I cannot turn back from my decision to go with Jesus wherever he goes. I believe in him and am willing to do anything for him."

Philip knew there was no use protesting further. Simon had told him what he intended to do. What could he say? Finally he asked, "When can I hear your Rabbi teach?"

"He will be in the synagogue tomorrow," replied Simon. "I am sure you will understand why I feel this way," he added very earnestly.

On Sabbath morning the streets which Philip had found so silent the evening before were filled with people. From every part of Capernaum they climbed to the place where the synagogue stood. It was on the highest hill in the city, because no building was more important to the people than their place of worship.

Simon and Philip came hurrying with the crowd. At the door of the synagogue they stopped to catch their breath and looked at the lake below them. The water lay still and smooth in the morning light, but no one knew better than the fishermen how quickly a wind storm could sweep down the ravines between the hills around the lake and whip up dangerous waves.

"Where is the Rabbi?" asked Philip.

"He is probably inside," answered Simon, turning to enter the synagogue.

From behind a row of pillars they looked for Jesus among the men who filled the room. In the middle of the room was a low platform with a desk on it. Seats were arranged on all sides. Over their heads was a balcony where the women sat. Simon pointed.

"There is Jesus down near the front," he whispered to Philip. "We'll sit with him." Philip noticed the tone of reverence in Simon's voice.

A row of dignified men sat in front of a heavy curtain at the end of the room. One of them came over to Jesus. Simon and Philip were too far away to hear what he whispered, but evidently he asked Jesus, as the visiting teacher, to take part in the service, because Jesus followed him and sat down with the elders. The synagogue filled quickly. Philip thought that many people must have heard about Jesus and come to Capernaum. Jesus walked to the desk on the platform. Philip was impressed by his strong voice repeating a prayer that was often used in the synagogue:

> "Blessed be Thou, O Lord, King of the world,
> Who formest the light and createst the darkness,
> Who in mercy givest light to the earth and to
> those who dwell upon it,
> And in Thy goodness, day by day and every day,
> renewest the works of creation.
> Blessed be the Lord our God for the glory of His
> handiworks,
> And for the light-giving lights which He has
> made for His praise. Selah."

In the second prayer, Jesus asked God to forgive and help
the people.

"With great love hast Thou loved us, O Lord our God,
And with much overflowing pity hast Thou pitied us,
Our Father and our King.
For the sake of our fathers who trusted in Thee,
And Thou taughtest them the statutes of life,
Have mercy upon us, and teach us.
Enlighten our eyes in Thy law;
Cause our hearts to cleave to Thy commandments:
Unite our hearts to love and fear Thy Name,
And we shall not be put to shame, world without end.
Amen."

Then all the congregation repeated their Creed in unison.

" 'Hear, O Israel: The Lord our God is one God. . . .
Thou shalt love the Lord thy God with all thy heart,
And with all thy soul,
And with all thy might.'
Remember all the commandments of the Lord and do
them.
'I am the Lord your God, who brought you . . . out of
the land of Egypt'
To be your God. I am the Lord your God."

Philip leaned over and whispered to Simon, "Do you think
he will dare say anything about founding a new kingdom?"

"I have never heard him here before," answered Simon, "but
he will say what he thinks."

After Jesus had repeated two prayers of thanksgiving, the
minister of the synagogue brought a heavy scroll to the desk. A
man from the congregation read some verses from Leviticus;
then several other men read short passages.

The people stirred expectantly when Jesus stood up. Again
Philip was impressed by the clear and convincing manner of his
speech. "Listen to the words of the Prophet Isaiah," Jesus said.

"The Spirit of the Lord is upon me, for he has consecrated
me to preach the gospel to the poor. He has sent me to proclaim release for captives and recovery of sight for the blind. He
has sent me to set free the oppressed and to proclaim the year of

the Lord's blessing." Jesus rolled up the scroll. Every person in the synagogue waited to hear what he would say.

"This very year," declared Jesus quietly but firmly, "is the year that Isaiah is talking about. You do not have to wait any longer for God to come to you. The words of Isaiah are true right now; God is here. The prophets tell you about a great day, but that day is not far in the future! God can be your King now! He can defeat every evil power. He will rule you if only you will open your hearts to him."

Philip turned to Simon. He was disappointed. "What can he mean by that?" Simon did not answer. He was waiting attentively for Jesus to go on.

"You think you are oppressed and poor," continued Jesus. "But I tell you that you will never win freedom by fighting and by shedding blood. Only the truth of God can make you free. Only his eternal treasures can make you rich! It is useless to depend on earthly things: moths destroy clothing; rust destroys iron; thieves steal money. Fire will burn down barns. Do not spend your lives getting things that pass away. Rather, store up treasures in the Kingdom of God. Only God's Kingdom is truly real. Only in his Kingdom are you truly free. Only his treasures make you really rich!"

"But how shall we get this Kingdom? That is what I want to know!" whispered Philip hoarsely to Simon.

"He will tell you," answered Simon.

"You spend all your time getting ready for a Kingdom that is far away," cried Jesus. "You do not have to wait for God's Kingdom. God is here now, working among you." His voice became stern. "The trouble is that you do not really believe in God at all. You do not wish to give yourselves to him. You always want to live for yourselves a little longer. You are blind to the rule of God because you are stubborn and unwilling to obey his will.

"The prophets tell you what God wants you to do! Have you obeyed them? No! Repent your sin! Give yourselves to God! On this very day you shall find his Kingdom!"

The people were looking at Jesus blankly. They had never heard anyone speak like this before. But Philip was able to understand one thing: the Kingdom of which Jesus had been speaking was very different from anything he had expected.

Behind them Simon and Philip heard a man say, "He doesn't speak as the scribes do!" Scribes always read or recited from memory the comments which the great Rabbis had written on the Law and the Prophets.

Suddenly there was a fearful scream in the rear of the building. A man had jumped from his bench near the back of the synagogue and was rushing down the aisle. Insanely he yelled: "Ha! Jesus of Nazareth! What business have you with me?"

"Let me out of here!" exclaimed a frightened man on the front benches. "He has a demon!" In his haste to get out of reach, the man tipped the bench over and it struck the stone floor with a bang.

"Have you come to destroy us?" shrieked the madman. "I know who you are! You are the Holy One from God!"

"Silence! Come out of him!" In an instant, Jesus had taken complete control of the man; as though all his strength suddenly melted away, he dropped to the floor and lay still. A single moan broke the tense silence of the synagogue. He seemed to be dying. Jesus motioned to the elders and they brought a cup of water.

In a moment the man stood up. He was weak but in his right mind. Utter amazement filled the people.

The elders were looking at one another, shaking their heads. "There is no doubt about it. He is free!" Others asked in wonder: "Who can this Rabbi be? He even has power over demons!"

People pressed toward the front of the room to stare at the man whom Jesus had healed. After a while, they began to drift away, talking excitedly. Philip did not push forward with the curious crowd but stood staring at Jesus. Even after the people had all gone, he continued to gaze wonderingly at Jesus. He could hardly believe his eyes: The man who had been so violent now sat quietly listening to Jesus.

Simon came over to where Philip was standing. "Do you now see how powerful his word is, Philip?" he asked. "Do you see why I follow him?"

"Never in all my life have I known such a man," said Philip, almost speaking to himself. He could not understand what was happening within him. He did not feel excited; his mind was clear and cool—but Philip knew that some strange power was at work. Everything had somehow changed. Jesus turned to him.

"Philip," asked the Master simply, "will you follow me?"

Jesus' words were like the turning of a key. Philip wanted to speak only words of obedience: "Master! I will go with you anywhere!"

4. GOD IS NOW KING!

BEFORE nightfall, all Capernaum was talking about the Teacher from Nazareth who had power to overcome demons. What strange person had arrived in their midst? He had even dared to break the Sabbath law, for healing on the day of rest was strictly forbidden. Some believed he was planning to start a rebellion to set the nation free from Roman rule; but to the sick and lame of Capernaum, the news meant just one thing: someone had come to help them.

Curious eyes had seen Jesus leave the synagogue with Simon. No sooner had the sun set, marking the end of the Sabbath, than hundreds of crippled and diseased persons crowded to the street where Simon lived. Jesus would not refuse them. In the cool twilight he taught and healed all who asked.

As it grew darker, the disciples began to marvel that the people kept coming. They knew everyone was very superstitious and hardly anyone ever went out at night for fear of evil spirits. But as the hours passed, Simon noticed many people who were not sick or crippled. They came for another kind of help; they knew Jesus could give more than healing for the body.

In the babble of voices Simon suddenly heard a man cry out sharply. The pain in the man's voice cut into Simon's heart like a knife. Simon scanned the crowd, but in the darkness could not see him. No one moved to let him through.

Jesus looked toward the man. "Do you cry out to me?" he asked, raising his voice above the noisy crowd around him. "Come and I will help you." Unwillingly, the people made way and the man crawled toward Jesus. Something was wrong with his legs. A hush settled over the crowd when Jesus spoke. "Your greatest need is not to be free from pain—it is to be rid of sin. Repent and turn back to God. Believe my word and you shall enter the Kingdom of God!" Jesus stooped and laid his hand on the man lying before him.

"O Father," he prayed, "heal this man of his suffering, in order that he may know thy truth and enter thy Kingdom." Jesus straightened up and held out his arms to all the people. "Come to me, all of you who labor and are heavy-laden, and I will give you rest!"

The disciples felt the power of their Master as they heard him call on the people to repent. They had never known anyone like him; they had never heard a message like his. Again and again they heard Jesus say: "Do you understand why you have been healed? This is a sign that the power of God has come among you."

It was after midnight when the last person left. Jesus was very tired. He looked at the black sky. There was no moon. The stars shed a faint light on the hills above Capernaum. Jesus turned to Simon. "It is time to rest." He went into the house.

"The people had no fear of evil night spirits," remarked James.

"They know he has power over them," commented Simon.

In the morning, long before dawn, Jesus rose in order to pray outside the city. A few yards from Simon's home the street dwindled to a path, and Jesus had to push through the stiff, dry grass which grew knee-high all over the hillside. As he climbed, he walked around large rocks. When he reached the crest of the hill, Jesus stood for a long while gazing down at Capernaum, barely visible in the starlight. There was a little breeze from the east. It smelled of both lake and desert.

The memory of the sick and lame people filled Jesus with sorrow. Some of these people really thought that everything would be all right if their bodies could be healed! What a terrible mistake! Had they understood what he had told them?

Would they realize that they were thinking only of themselves? Perhaps their lives were too cluttered with little hopes and ambitions to see the will of God. How dearly they loved worthless things! Jesus found a hollow where the bushes sheltered him from the wind and knelt to pray.

Dawn was turning the gray sky to blue when Simon was aroused from sleep by the noise of a crowd outside his house. He dressed hastily.

"Where is the Healer?" shouted the people. Simon waved his hand for silence.

"He is not here." His words were instantly drowned by a hundred voices. "Where is he?" everyone demanded at once.

"I don't know where he is," answered Simon.

"Will he be back? Where did he go?"

Simon knew he would never succeed in sending them away. Andrew came out of the house.

"Do you think we could find him?" asked Simon.

"We can try," answered Andrew, smiling wryly. Without explaining their plan to the people, they set out toward the hills. Some of the people tried to follow, but Simon gruffly sent them back.

The two men followed a faint path toward the top of the hill. For about a mile they walked, searching the slopes on both sides of them. "We may not find him at all," remarked Simon. At that moment Andrew caught sight of a patch of white ahead of them.

"Is he up there?"

Simon began to run. Jesus was kneeling in prayer. Andrew had seen a corner of his woolen robe against the dark bushes.

"Rabbi!" panted Simon. "Everyone is looking for you!"

He had interrupted Jesus' prayer, but Jesus was not offended. "I am not going back to Capernaum."

"But, Rabbi," protested Simon, "hundreds of people need you. They are in pain. What will they do without you?"

"I must go to the other villages of Galilee and preach the news of the Kingdom there too," replied Jesus.

"But, Master, your word is the only help these people have ever had." He realized that Jesus had fully made up his mind to go. "Think of the blind and the crippled!" he cried desperately. "What will become of them?"

Jesus answered with firm conviction. "Simon, they have heard the news that God has come to them. I have a greater work than healing the sick bodies—my work is to proclaim to everyone the message which gives them a whole new life! This is why God has sent me! I must go on to the cities of Galilee!"

Simon and Andrew knew they could not change their Rabbi's mind, so at his command they returned to Capernaum and prepared for a trip through Galilee. At noon the disciples left Capernaum, carrying only a small amount of food, and met Jesus outside the city. Jesus knew it was hard for Simon to leave his wife and children.

By late afternoon they had reached Tarichaea, a town smaller than Capernaum, about six miles south on the shore of the Lake of Galilee. Here lived many rich men who owned the fertile farms on which all Galilee depended for wheat. There was also a large fish business, because in Tarichaea fish were salted and sold to men who came to buy food for the Roman army.

The market place was busy when Jesus arrived with the disciples, and a group of people quickly gathered to hear him teach. A young man in fine clothing joined the circle around Jesus. The disciples immediately recognized that he was a member of the party of the Pharisees because he wore large tassels on his robe. During a pause in the discussion he asked a question which Simon thought must have been troubling him for some time.

"Good Teacher," he asked, "you have told these others how to enter the Kingdom of God. Now what must I do to inherit eternal life?"

Jesus looked at the young man keenly. "Why do you call me 'good'?" he asked. "Only God is good." Then his tone softened. "You know the commandments—do not commit adultery; do not kill; do not steal; do not speak lies—if you obey the law of God you possess eternal life."

The disciples looked at the young man with the greatest respect. Here was a really religious man! A Pharisee who kept all the Law—what more could God require? And he was rich. Did that not prove he had pleased God?

"But, Teacher," replied the young man, "I have obeyed every one of these laws perfectly since I was a child. But somehow . . . it is not enough. I am not satisfied."

John was puzzled. *This man should be happy,* he thought. *I was just a poor fisherman, but this man seems to have everything.* The other disciples also wondered what Jesus could say to the young man.

"You lack just one thing," said Jesus. "You must get rid of all your possessions. Sell your property. Go and give your money to the poor. Come and be my disciple."

Shock and disappointment came over the young man's face. "I can't do a thing like that!" he exclaimed. "Why should I give my money away?"

"You must sell all that you have and give to the poor," insisted Jesus. "If you want eternal life, you must put God first. If you go on clinging to the things you own, no matter how little you may keep back, you will never find the Kingdom of God."

"But God gave me my money," protested the young Pharisee. "Is he not the one who gives all good things? Why should you ask me to get rid of things he himself has given me?" The disciples felt that his argument was logical. "I have kept every detail of the religious rules," continued the young man. "I even keep two fasts instead of one! I never break the Sabbath. Don't you think I have earned eternal life?"

Jesus answered simply; he did not argue. "Any man who wishes to enter the Kingdom must seek the will of God above every other goal. Where a man's treasure is, there is his heart also. You have not given yourself to Him. You trust in your possessions and in your good deeds."

This is unreasonable! thought the young man. He turned and left. Yet the longing to be sure he had pleased God was strong still. "That is no solution!" he insisted, arguing within himself. "God cannot ask me to give up things he has given me. People turn from sins—not from their good deeds!" But he could not forget Jesus' demand: "Repent! You love your own riches more than you love God. Repent!"

Jesus looked sorrowfully after the young man. "How difficult it is for a rich man to enter the Kingdom!" he exclaimed regretfully. "It is easier for a camel to go through the eye of a needle than for a rich man to give himself to God!"

The disciples listened astonished. Finally Simon blurted out: "But, Master, if he cannot be saved, who can? He is a good man!"

Jesus answered with the deepest feeling: "Simon, with man it is impossible. But with God—all things are possible!"

"Well," said Simon, "if giving up things is the answer, we ought to have eternal life. We have given up everything!" There was bitterness in his voice, and everyone knew he was thinking of his children in Capernaum.

Jesus felt great sympathy for Simon, and his answer was very gentle. "Yes, Simon, you have given up much. But you need not fear—a man who gives up his home and his property for my sake will never be sorry. He will receive back a hundred times over the eternal gifts which God gives those who love him. Many who now are rich will be the last in God's Kingdom; but those who are poor for my sake will be the very first in his Kingdom!"

That night the disciples stayed in Tarichaea. They did not argue any more about what Jesus had told the rich Pharisee, but they were more troubled by these words than by anything else Jesus had said. His teachings seemed against everything they had ever learned!

The next day, as the band of men walked with Jesus toward Nazareth, Simon brought up the question. "Teacher," he said earnestly, "I don't understand why you talked to that young

Pharisee as you did. He was very sincere. The Pharisees do more to obey God than any others and this young man looked to me as though he tried even harder than most. God had even given him riches as a reward for his goodness! And yet you said he had to get rid of all his wealth in order to enter the Kingdom of Heaven!" Simon could hardly find words to express his strong feelings. "I needed to repent, but why should he? He was already a good man!"

James summed up the thoughts of them all: "Rabbi, if a man as good as that can't enter the Kingdom, how can anyone?"

Jesus said: "Simon, I want to tell you a story. Two men went up to the Temple to pray. One was a Pharisee—like the young man we talked with yesterday. The other was a tax collector, who had been dishonest.

"The Pharisee stood by himself, a distance away from the ordinary folk who went in and out of the Temple, and prayed this way: 'God, I thank thee that I am not like other men—thieves, rogues, and immoral—like that taxgatherer over there. You know I am a good man. I fast twice a week and pay tithes of all my money.'

"But the taxgatherer," continued Jesus, "went off in a corner where he could hide from people. He wouldn't even lift up his eyes as he prayed. Rather, he hung his head and beat his breast in the deepest shame and said, 'God, be merciful to me, a sinner!' "

The disciples did not seem to understand, so Jesus said: "The taxgatherer left the Temple accepted by God. But not the Pharisee! He trusted in his own goodness rather than in God. If he had been humble, like the taxgatherer, God could have forgiven him."

"But I don't see what that has to do with the young Pharisee," protested James. "He was not dishonest! Why should he be ashamed?"

"This young ruler was like the Pharisee in the Temple," replied Jesus. "He was so confident of his own goodness that he could not see how far he was from what God wants him to be."

"But, Master," urged Simon, "look at the things that the Pharisees do! They educate our children in religion in the synagogue schools. They never have anything to do with the Sadducees or priests who take money from the Romans. They study the Scriptures more than anyone else; don't these things count for anything?"

"Men may do all these things and yet have no real faith in God," answered Jesus. "The Kingdom of Heaven comes to men who love God above everything else. There was something that meant more to that young man yesterday than God—and that was his money. Other men depend on other things; whatever they are, they must get rid of them. Even the most upright Pharisee must forget his pride in goodness and trust God as simply as a little child."

John shook his head doubtfully. "The people will never understand that," he said. "Even though the Pharisees are often very snobbish, they are the best people in our nation."

Jesus suddenly became grim. "The whole religion of the Pharisees sets them against the Kingdom of Heaven!"

The men looked at him in surprise. "But Master," urged James, "we need them to help us set up the new Kingdom! They are more loyal to God than anyone else. Besides, we can do nothing without their friendship."

"I know them, James," answered Jesus. "Men who are sure of themselves will never welcome what we have to tell them!"

John shook his head but said no more. This was not his idea of the way the Kingdom would come. The disciples felt sure Jesus could not mean all he said. But two days later they realized they were wrong. Jesus had meant every word.

After a short trip through lower Galilee, the men arrived in Nazareth where Jesus had lived until a few months before. His mother and brothers were still there, but Jesus stayed outside the town until Sabbath morning and then went with them to the synagogue.

The rumors of Jesus' miracles had spread through all Galilee, and when Jesus entered the synagogue many people looked at him curiously. He saw many people he knew. There was the woman who had lived next to them for twenty years and who was a special friend of his mother's; there were several young men whom he knew well. He smiled across the congregation at one young man who had helped him in the carpenter shop after his father Joseph had died, when Jesus was forced to support the family.

The minister of the synagogue, an old friend of Jesus', invited him to lead the service. After the prayers, he sat down at the desk in the center of the synagogue and opened the scroll to the Prophet Isaiah.

Looking into the faces of many people who had known him from boyhood, Jesus knew it would not be easy to tell them about the Kingdom. He read the same passage he had read in Capernaum: "The Spirit of the Lord is upon me, for he has consecrated me to preach the gospel to the poor. He has sent me to proclaim release for captives and recovery of sight for the blind. He has sent me to set free the oppressed and to proclaim the year of the Lord's blessing."

Jesus rolled up the scroll. Everyone waited for him to speak. "Today," he declared, "these words of the Prophet Isaiah have come true right here. God has sent his Holy Spirit upon me to tell you that he is now among you. If you truly know that you need God, your ears will be open to hear this word from him; but if you are proud, you will be deaf. Put your entire trust in God and seek his will! I declare to you that God's Kingdom is not far in the future; God has brought it to your door!"

He paused and looked from person to person. "Who would have thought Joseph's son would turn out so well?" whispered one of the elders to a neighbor.

"He does speak with ease," replied his friend, a grudging note in his voice.

"If we could see him do a miracle, we should know for sure whether he is all he claims," said the elder.

From the very first, Jesus had known that the people of Nazareth would find it hard to believe in him. Looking at the elders, he said: "No doubt you are ready to say to me, 'Do for us here in your own home town the things you have been doing in Capernaum.' But prophets are never accepted by the people of their own country. There were many Jewish widows who needed Elijah's help when the great famine came over all Israel, but God did not send him to any of them—they would not believe in him. He sent him to a widow in Sidon, a gentile!

"Elisha could have found many Jewish lepers who needed to be healed, but not one of them was made clean. They would not believe in him! Rather, he healed Naaman, a Syrian and a gentile!"

A deathly silence settled over the synagogue. They were not as good as gentiles! Gentiles, who were unclean outsiders! A carpenter's son telling them that God would pass them by for gentiles! The men began to murmur angrily. Jesus' voice rang out: "How can I do great deeds among you when you do not really believe God at all?"

Open anger swept through the synagogue. "How dare he talk like this to us?" demanded one man, leaping to his feet. All over the room men began to crowd toward the front where Jesus stood.

"Let us have order here!" The minister could hardly make his voice heard. A group of men rushed toward Jesus, who did not even step back. "Over the cliff with him!" shouted someone. In a moment they were shoving and hustling Jesus toward the door, yelling, "Over the cliff with him!"

Carrying Jesus with them, the crowd moved swiftly toward a place outside the town where the hill dropped straight down. Then a peculiar thing happened. The men seemed suddenly to realize what they were doing. This was Mary's son! The son of Joseph, the carpenter who for many years had made yokes for their oxen.

Wrath seemed to melt away. The men let go of Jesus' robe. They seemed almost afraid of him. None laid a hand on him as he walked through the mob which only a moment before had wanted to kill him.

An instant after Jesus was gone, anger again came over the men like the backwash from an ocean wave. Some shook their fists in the direction Jesus had gone, but not one had the courage to follow.

The disciples did not attempt to follow Jesus. They were glad that no one in the town knew them, and they wasted no time in leaving. They all realized that men who were afraid of Jesus might take out their anger on his followers. It was late that night before the disciples found one another and started to hunt for their Master.

Jesus had left the city and climbed to a high ridge where he had loved to go as a boy. Now he looked down on the broad valley of Esdraelon, stretching south to the foothills of Samaria, where so many of the great battles of ancient Israel had been fought. Had he not always felt that someday he would be rejected by his own home town?

Nevertheless, Jesus was not scorned by everyone in Nazareth. A few people remembered the place he loved and they came to him there. They were not rich people, and there were no elders from the synagogue among them. They were the sick and crippled; they were people for whom life was hard, and they believed the word which Jesus had spoken to them. The disciples found him teaching and healing these few.

"These have heard my word," said Jesus to the followers. "To them the Kingdom is given." The disciples listened to Jesus telling the poorest folk of Nazareth the news of the Kingdom. When they left, Jesus spoke very plainly to the disciples.

"Why are you so discouraged?" he asked. "Have we not preached the gospel of the Kingdom here?"

"They turned us out!" burst out James. "They laughed at us! They tried to kill you!"

Simon was bitter. "We should never come near this miserable village again. We might have been killed!"

"If men are to enter the Kingdom of God, they must repent," answered Jesus. "It cuts them to the heart to confess that they have forgotten God and his righteousness. They hate us for teaching them the truth about themselves."

The disciples sat in gloomy silence. Simon gazed out over the plains below. Here through many defeats in battle the Jews had paid the price of their sin—but Israel had not yet learned. Still the nation spurned the prophets whom God sent. Would the Kingdom never come?

5. WHO IS THIS CARPENTER?

AFTER their harsh experience at Nazareth, the disciples were prepared for other disappointments. Before they entered the next town on their journey through Galilee the men talked soberly, a little fearfully, about what might happen. But, one after another, the villages of Galilee welcomed Jesus. The common people listened eagerly to the news that he proclaimed, and many believed. The disciples began to forget that Jesus had been driven out of Nazareth.

Late one Friday afternoon just before the Sabbath began, Jesus led the disciples into Chorazin, a town crowded in by the steep walls of a valley north of Capernaum. A full hour before sunset the hills to the west threw deep shadows over the village. It was cooler than Capernaum, thought Simon. Soon he would be home with his wife and children! But he was as glad as the others to rest in Chorazin over the Sabbath. They had traveled all week, pausing only to tell the good news in the towns they had passed through, and they were very tired.

The men rose the next morning greatly refreshed, ready to worship at the synagogue. They were sure Jesus would be asked to teach. Most of the disciples expected the people to receive Jesus gladly, but Simon could not forget the last time they had been in a synagogue—at Nazareth. It was in the market places and on the streets, Simon remembered, not in the synagogues, that Jesus had been most gladly welcomed.

As soon as they entered the synagogue, Simon decided that the whole town must have seen them arrive the night before; everyone was expecting them. Invited by the minister of the synagogue, Jesus took his place behind the desk on the low platform in the center of the room, and read from the Prophets. Then he told the people very plainly that God was among them in great power; that they must immediately give up everything that kept them from understanding God's purpose and devote their lives to him. Both the people and the elders listened closely, and Simon was not surprised when many people gathered around Jesus as soon as the service was over. The minister and the elders asked many serious questions, and Simon saw that they were very sincere. The things Jesus had said disturbed them deeply. No one noticed a very short woman quietly walking up behind the men who surrounded Jesus.

When at last there were no more questions, Jesus turned to go. The men stepped back. For the first time, Jesus saw the woman. Shyly she moved away. Instantly he realized why she had come. Her back was terribly bent.

"Do not be afraid," he said to her encouragingly; "come here!" She hesitated.

Does he realize that this is the Sabbath? Simon thought in alarm.

As though he were alone with the woman, Jesus laid his hand on her twisted back and raised his eyes in prayer: "Father, I thank thee that thou hearest me when I pray. Set this woman free, I beseech thee, from the deformity which has bent her body these many years. This I ask in order that she may know that thou hast sent me with thy message of life." While Jesus was praying, Simon glanced at the elders of the synagogue.

They were utterly amazed at what Jesus was doing. *Doesn't this Nazarene know this is the Sabbath?* wondered the minister.

Jesus had finished. He said, "You are freed from your infirmity." She stood up straight. "May God be praised!" she exclaimed. There were tears of joy in her eyes.

"God's blessing on you, Rabbi!" The woman's friends had been watching from the balcony and now they ran down to the main floor of the synagogue and gathered around her.

Amazed and outraged, the minister looked from the woman to Jesus and back again. Angrily he turned to the people. "The Law says there are six days in each week for work. That means there are six days for getting healed. What more do you need? Why do you come on the Sabbath?"

Simon glanced at Jesus and almost shivered. Jesus had seen the distress and embarrassment of the woman. "You hypocrite!" The man cringed. He had not imagined Jesus would dare speak to him like this. "Do you scold this woman for coming to be healed on the Sabbath? Every single one of you will lead your ox to water as soon as you get home. If that isn't work, what is?" His scorn bit into the elders like a whiplash. "You say the Law allows you to give your cattle water. Hasn't this woman the right to be healed? For eighteen years her body has been twisted. She is a child of Abraham! Isn't she more important than any animal?" Jesus looked right through the men. They felt like fish wriggling on a spear.

The friends of the woman stole triumphant glances at the elders. Simon knew Jesus was getting into trouble, but it made no difference: his Master was right!

Without another word, Jesus strode out of the synagogue. The people left in the room felt suddenly cold, and all but the elders hastened away to their homes.

Hardly wishing to look at one another, the elders sighed and sat down. It was not just that they were angry. They were baffled by what Jesus had said. Their respect for the Sabbath rule was sincere; they believed it was the most important regulation in the entire Jewish Law. No one who disobeyed it, they were certain, could possibly love God. "Never in my life have I seen such a fanatic!" exclaimed the minister finally.

"He is dangerous," agreed another. "What will happen to our religion if the people begin to think that they don't need to keep the Sabbath?"

"We must tell the people how serious a matter this is," said the minister. "I am going down to Capernaum tomorrow. I will stop and talk to our friend Symeon. He may know about this Jesus. Perhaps he can tell us what we ought to do."

At the inn where they were staying, the disciples were gloomy and silent. They were worried about the dispute with the elders; but they were troubled also about the thing Jesus had done that morning. Jesus knew that he had perplexed them, and he was not surprised when the next day, on the road down to Capernaum, Simon spoke up.

"Master, we would like to ask a question," said Simon. The others gathered closely around. "Moses told us at Mount Sinai, 'Remember the sabbath day, to keep it holy.' He told us never to work on the Sabbath. Yet, Rabbi, you healed the woman on the Sabbath. We *do* believe she is more important than any animal—but still, Rabbi, you did break the Sabbath rule! Do you want the Sabbath forgotten? Do you intend to cast out all the laws and rules?" Simon's tense voice told Jesus he was deeply disturbed. The other disciples looked at Jesus gravely.

"I have not come to destroy the Law," he answered. "Rather, I am showing you what it really means to obey the Law."

"But you did heal the hunchbacked woman on the Sabbath, didn't you?" persisted Simon.

"Unless you obey the Law better than these men who make the Sabbath so important, you can never enter the Kingdom of Heaven," replied Jesus.

"We don't think they are right, Master," explained Simon. "We think that the woman was more important than the animals, which they feed and water on the Sabbath. But . . ." Jesus knew Simon was not satisfied.

"Even though the Pharisees are very careful about little

things," said Jesus, "that does not mean that they know what God asks of them. They obey the Sabbath rule—but inwardly they have forgotten justice and mercy. They all know that it is wrong to kill another Jew. But much more is required than that: if you even hold a grudge against another person, you have no right to pray to God. The Pharisees give much attention to small rules and forget the important things."

"This seems so new," said Simon. "I don't understand very well."

"I have only told you what Moses and the Prophets taught," replied Jesus. "The meaning of their words has been forgotten, even though the Pharisees talk about them a great deal."

"But don't you think we are likely to get into trouble if we speak out like this in public?" urged Andrew. "We can teach the people, but I don't think we need to be so harsh with the Pharisees and the elders of the synagogues. We ought to be careful. The Pharisees are really good people and we must not offend them. How can we preach the good news to the people if we do? When we go to the synagogues, I think it is much safer to keep quiet."

Jesus watched the men listening to Andrew and knew why they agreed. He knew the inward emptiness of fear—fear of a future they could not know. Andrew was right; their peril was increasing every day. But Jesus shook his head. "My followers," he said, "do not think that I was sent to bring peace to this nation. I came to bring strife. It cannot be any other way. Men enter the Kingdom of God only through conflict and pain."

When the disciples arrived in Capernaum on the day after the Sabbath, they heard a report that dismayed them: John the Baptizer had been thrown into prison by King Herod. They found out about it through one of his followers who had come to Capernaum to find Jesus and was waiting for them at Simon's home. The man's name was Jacob. Andrew and John remembered him as one of the Baptizer's most loyal disciples.

"What made the king do it?" asked Andrew.

"John told the king he was doing wrong in the sight of God," replied Jacob.

John is no bolder than Jesus, thought Andrew.

Jacob added, "John himself told us just before he was taken prisoner that we should come to you."

Andrew turned to Jesus. "What will Herod do to him?"

"There is no way to tell. We must be prepared to hear the worst."

"Why did John send you to us?" Simon asked Jacob.

"Some of us went to him and told him that more people were following your Master than were following him," answered the man. "He just said to us: 'Didn't I tell you that I am not the Christ? I am glad that Jesus has many followers. He must grow even stronger, and I must decrease.' When he was thrown into prison, I came to you."

Andrew looked at Jesus and spoke the thought in the minds of them all: "If we go on proclaiming the gospel, the same thing may happen to us."

Jesus' answer was firm: "Nothing must stand in our way. We speak for God."

Never before had the men felt the strength of Jesus as they did now. There was not a trace of fear in his actions. He knew that their danger was increasing every day! And he acted with such authority! Everything he said or did proved that he knew what he was about. It was his certainty that convinced the people!

An event occurred on the second day of their return to Capernaum which showed the disciples that they might soon share the fate of John the Baptizer. It did not take many hours for the report to spread through all Capernaum that Jesus was back in the city. From every corner of the town came those needing help—not only the sick and lame, but people of all kinds who were restless and dissatisfied. So many people crowded into the courtyard of Simon's home that Jesus decided to stand in the doorway of his room where he could see them all. The porch roof shaded him. He was about to raise his hand to quiet the people when Andrew hurried to him.

"Master," he whispered excitedly, "there are Pharisees and their scribes outside."

"Well, bring them in."

Andrew was amazed. "But, Master, some of them are from Jerusalem!"

Jesus knew what that meant. Over the crowd he caught Simon's eye. The fisherman was worried. *From Jerusalem!* Simon was thinking. *They have come to see if what we are teaching is against the Law of Moses.*

Jesus realized that news of his preaching must have traveled to Jerusalem. He knew that officials of the Pharisees would come to hear him personally. He expected no friendliness from them; but he was ready.

He glanced behind him. "There is room for them there. Bring them in."

Andrew looked anxiously at Jesus. "O Master, don't . . ."

Jesus looked at him. "Courage, Andrew! Make certain that they see and hear everything that happens."

People stepped back respectfully as the scribes and Pharisees came in. Jesus paid no special attention. He had turned to the people who stood before him.

"I have been sent by God with news," he began. "If you are poor, you can be rich if you will humble your heart and trust God."

He saw a man covered with sores. "Are you unclean?" he said, looking at him. "God will accept you. You are clean in his sight if your heart is turned toward him.

"Are you full of fears and worries? Come unto me, all of you that are burdened in spirit, and I will give you rest."

There were many outside the house who could not get in because there was no room. Among them were four men carrying a stretcher. On it lay a man who was helpless from paralysis. His body had wasted away to skin and bone. His four friends had heard about Jesus' power, but now they stood in front of the house in dismay.

"We can never get in," said one.

"There's no use waiting until they leave," said another.

"Let's take him back," said the first, discouraged.

"No indeed!" The others were determined. "I am sure he will

be healed if we can just find some way to get through," said one of them.

The fourth man was gazing at a staircase that led up to the roof of the house next to Simon's home.

"Look! Why can't we get in that way?"

In a moment the men had climbed the stairs and stepped across the narrow space that separated them from the roof of Simon's house. On the porch under them, they could hear Jesus talking. It took about fifteen minutes to lift the tile from the porch roof, tie ropes to the stretcher, and lower the man toward Jesus.

Everybody stared as the paralyzed man slowly came to rest at the feet of Jesus.

"My son!" Jesus' voice could be clearly heard in the hush of the courtyard. "Your sins are forgiven."

The statement took everyone by surprise. Andrew saw a scribe whisper to a friend.

"Did you hear what he said?" remarked the scribe whom Andrew was watching. His friend nodded.

A woman who knew the sick man said: "Is this man paralyzed because he sinned? He was born this way, wasn't he?"

"He has been a very good man," answered her husband.

Jesus turned to the scribes and Pharisees. "Why are you wondering about what I said? Tell me which is easier, to say to this man, 'Your sins are forgiven,' or to say, 'Rise, take up your pallet and walk'?"

None tried to speak. Then Jesus said, " 'But that you may know that the Son of man has authority on earth to forgive sins' "—he turned to the sick man—"Get up! Pick up your bed and carry it away!"

Strength surged into the wasted frame of the paralytic. He rose and did as Jesus told him. A whisper ran over the crowd.

The Pharisees and scribes sat silent. Watching them carefully, Simon saw that they were puzzled. An elderly man, who appeared to be a leader, whispered to a friend, "He actually claims to forgive sin! God alone can do that."

The Pharisees and scribes rose to leave. They walked through the crowd without looking at the people. When they were outside, the elderly leader shook his head very gravely. "I had hoped this man would be a friend of the Law, but I am afraid he is not. 'Your sins are forgiven!' What a blasphemous thing for a man to dare to say!"

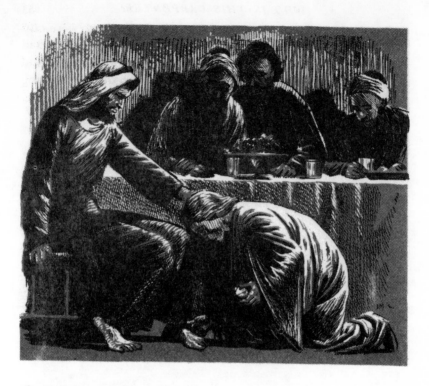

6. THE OLD AND THE NEW

"RABBI, it is a serious mistake for us to mix with outcasts!"
Simon was disturbed. Jesus had summoned a tax collector
named Levi to follow him. On this night the tax collector had
asked Jesus and his disciples to come to his home for dinner. "I
know that Levi is different now," protested Simon, "but we
ought not to get mixed up with his old cronies. We should take
him away from that class of people!"

Jesus came straight to the point. "Don't you want to eat at
Levi's home at all?"

"No!" Simon answered bluntly. "After all, look who he is! A
taxgatherer! A traitor to our nation! For my part, I want nothing to do with him." Simon realized that his tone was not respect-
ful. "I am thinking of our work, Master. People will not listen
to us if we eat with those men. The best people will look down
on us!"

"Levi has sinned," answered Jesus. "That is why we called him to join us. His friends have sinned. We are going to eat with them because they need help. And do not forget, Simon, you will be judged by the same measuring stick that you use on Levi's friends."

"I am far from perfect, Rabbi," persisted Simon, "but I try to obey the Law." His tone became bitter. "Anyway, I never worked for King Herod! I cannot stand the idea of sitting down at the same table with tax collectors. It might as well be a gang of robbers!"

"Simon," said Jesus sternly, "before you start looking for the sliver in Levi's eye you had better dig the tree trunk out of your own." Strongly rebuked, Simon consented to eat with Levi and his friends, but he was very unwilling.

The next day two close friends of Symeon, the most respected citizen of Capernaum, stopped to visit him. The report of what Jesus had done came up.

"What I cannot understand," remarked Symeon, a dignified man of about sixty, "is how a man who wants to teach religion can actually associate with such people."

"For that matter," replied one of his friends, "look at the men who follow him. They are very common people—fishermen, this tax collector, and such like—not a Pharisee among them. Not one of them takes religion seriously."

"And yet I have heard this Nazarene myself," continued Symeon. "He says many things that show he knows the Law very well. He knows he should not eat with people like that Levi!"

"Did you hear about the healing at the fisherman's house the other day?" inquired the younger of the two visiting Pharisees. "Some men put a paralytic in front of the Nazarene while he was teaching. The first thing he said was, 'Your sins are forgiven.'" The others nodded.

"The puzzling thing is that this young teacher seems very sincere," said Symeon. "He really knows a great deal—and no one can deny that he has great power. The people go out to hear him everywhere. I want to find out his purpose. I have a suggestion that may help us see what he is trying to do." The other men looked up. "You may think this is going a little too far, but I should like to ask him to come to my house."

"But he is not a keeper of the Law!" protested the young Pharisee. "We should be as bad as he is, if we were to eat with him."

Symeon nodded. "I realize that it will not be easy for you, but I think we should do it. If there is something good in this Nazarene, we should know it. If he is up to mischief . . . Anyhow, I don't see how we can understand him unless we talk to him." The others said nothing, and Symeon took their silence for consent. "Of course," he added, "we will not invite the others —the fishermen and that tax collector. That would be too much! But I think it would be all right to have the Nazarene here just once."

When Jesus told the disciples that he was going to the home of Symeon, Andrew was pleased. "I guess we have not offended the Pharisees too badly after all," he exclaimed enthusiastically.

Simon too was relieved. "I hope, Master," he said, "that you will explain why we ate with Levi."

Jesus said very little. It was natural for fishermen and workers to want the approval of the most respected citizens of Capernaum. Yet Jesus knew how little the Pharisees cared for people like his own disciples.

There were many guests in Symeon's home, for this was the season of the New Year and every Jew left the door of his home open for any visitor who cared to enter. During the meal, both friends and strangers continued to come into the room, but Symeon was listening intently to Jesus as they conversed about religion.

"The men who obeyed God in past times were not the rich and the powerful," Jesus was saying. "Very often our nation has listened to God's voice only after defeat in war. When men know they are weak, they turn to God."

"Is this your purpose in going about and preaching to the people of Galilee?" asked Symeon. Everyone listened for the answer.

"I am sent to tell our people that God is their rightful King. His power is present among us," answered Jesus plainly. "But most of you will not take my message seriously. You trust other gods, and your hearts are hard."

The Pharisees looked at one another. Some were puzzled, others offended. "But surely you misunderstand us. We keep the Law very carefully," said Symeon.

"If you are really a teacher sent from God, how can you mix with outcasts?" The young Pharisee's question was blunt.

"I am not here to call the righteous to repent," answered Jesus, his eyes accusing the young man. "I am here to call sinners!" Irony came into his voice. "People who are healthy don't need a doctor. It is the sick who need help. It is to them that I am sent."

The room was tense, but before anyone could ask another question, Symeon's attention was drawn away. He glanced around the room. It sounded as though someone were weeping! He examined the shadowy corners where the light of the candles did not reach. At that moment a woman stepped swiftly toward Jesus and dropped to her knees.

Jesus turned and looked at her. He had not known she was hiding in the darkness behind him. Her tears fell on his feet. She loosed the cord that tied her hair. With its long waves she gently wiped Jesus' feet.

Symeon, usually dignified, was irritated. "What kind of nonsense is this?" he asked as he rose from his couch.

Jesus turned to him. "Do not rebuke her," he requested. *That is the trouble with leaving the door open,* thought Symeon. *Women like this are bound to get in.* Everyone there knew her. She had a bad reputation in the city. Symeon felt humiliated to have such a person in his house. *This Nazarene certainly knows all the worst people,* reflected the young Pharisee cynically.

Suddenly a lovely fragrance filled the room. The woman had broken open a bottle of precious perfume and recklessly poured every drop on Jesus' feet.

Such waste! thought Symeon angrily, realizing what she had done. *I wonder if the Nazarene has any idea where she got the money to buy this oil!* But he said nothing because he was very polite.

Jesus turned to his host. "Symeon," he said, "I have something to say to you."

"What is it, Teacher?" asked the Pharisee.

"There was once a man who loaned money," said Jesus. "One of his debtors owed him two hundred and fifty dollars; another owed him twenty-five dollars." The guests were listening closely. "Neither of these men could pay back the money, so the lender said to both of them: 'I forgive you your debts. You don't need to pay me back at all.' " He paused and then asked, "Now which of these two men would be more grateful?"

"Why, naturally, the man who owed more money would be more grateful," replied Symeon without hesitating.

"Right!" said Jesus. "When I came into your house you didn't even offer to wash my feet—and everyone does that for his guest! But this woman has washed my feet with her tears and dried them with her hair!

"You didn't welcome me with a kiss—and everyone greets his guest that way!" He pointed to the woman. "But she has been kissing my feet.

"You didn't anoint my head with oil—and everyone does that for his guest! But this woman has poured precious perfume on my feet!" Jesus' voice was quiet, but all the Pharisees could sense the force of his words when he said: "She has committed many sins, but they are all forgiven and now her heart is full of love." Then Jesus spoke directly to Symeon and each word seemed to strike him like a blow. "But a man whose sins are not forgiven has no love in his heart." Then he said very gently to the woman, "Your sins are forgiven."

Symeon's face burned hot. Never had anyone spoken like this to him! He was troubled by the suggestion that he was a sinner. All his life he had done his best to obey the Law. Had he not always prided himself on his good actions?

Hurt and confused, Symeon heard a friend beside him whisper, "Did you hear him say that this woman's sins are forgiven?" Abruptly Symeon looked up at the man. He was right! It was an outrage for anyone to say such a thing as this!

"You have no reason to be sorrowful," Jesus was saying to the woman. "Your faith has saved you."

Symeon stood up, his shame forgotten. Why had he ever let this person disturb him? Anyone who talked this way was a heretic and a blasphemer, nothing better! Only God could forgive sin. They all knew the truth about this Jesus now: such a man was dangerous to all true religion. As a Pharisee who loved the Law, he would have to do all he could to keep him from deceiving the people.

Jesus said nothing to the disciples about the events of the evening in Symeon's house. But two days later, while buying food, Andrew and John heard a rumor which they discovered later came from Symeon. "Should we tell the Master?" wondered John.

"We must." Andrew was positive. They made a quick trip to Simon's home, left their food, and hurried out to the shore of the lake. As usual, a large group of listeners surrounded Jesus. "We shall have to wait until we can talk to him alone," said Andrew.

A man whom the disciples had never seen before was questioning Jesus. "Rabbi, why do the Pharisees and the followers of John the Baptizer fast while your disciples pay no attention to the fasting rule?" Andrew and John exchanged startled glances; this was it!

Jesus answered very clearly. "Tell me," he asked, "do the friends of people who are getting married fast on the wedding day?"

"Of course not. That is a time for rejoicing, not fasting."

"Right," answered Jesus. "While the bridegroom is with his friends they are not sorrowful. But a time comes when he leaves them. There is time enough then to fast."

"But, Rabbi," protested the man, "the Pharisees say it is a serious sin not to fast."

"Listen to what I say," said Jesus. "If you have an old coat with a hole in it, do you patch it with a brand-new piece of cloth?"

"No, of course not."

"Why not?" asked Jesus.

"As soon as the new piece is wet by the rain," answered a woman very quickly, "it shrinks and tears the cloth of the old coat."

Jesus said, "If you try to add something new to the old, the new destroys the old, doesn't it?"

"What do you mean by that?" asked the first man after a moment's thought.

"Listen again. When you make new wine, do you pour it right into a dry, stiff wineskin that has been used before?" The people stored wine in whole goatskins, tied up tightly at the legs and neck.

"Of course not."

"Why not?"

"Because as soon as the wine begins to ferment it stretches the skin tight. New wine is powerful enough to rip an old bag to pieces!"

"Do you understand now what I am telling you?" asked Jesus. "Never try to put new wine in old skins. The old cannot hold the new. The gospel of the Kingdom of God asks you to do much more than just keep the fasts."

"The Pharisees don't say that," said the man doubtfully. "I don't know who is right. It is a serious thing not to keep the Law of Moses."

"Do you know what you remind me of?" Jesus said. "I saw some children in the market this morning who couldn't decide what they wanted to do. Some wanted to play that they were at a wedding; others, that they were at a funeral. When they piped wedding music, the ones who wanted a funeral wouldn't dance. And when they piped funeral music, the others quit. It was impossible to please them all.

"You and your teachers are like children who are never satisfied. John the Baptizer came and fasted often—and you said he had a demon. Now I come eating and drinking like other men and you call me a glutton and a drunkard. You accuse me of being friendly with tax collectors and other sinners. But what we do will prove to be right!"

When the crowd broke up, Andrew and John walked back to Capernaum with Jesus. "Someone had been talking to the man who asked that question," declared Andrew.

"Yes, I know," answered Jesus. "We must expect the Pharisees to criticize us. How careful they are to keep every little command of the rabbis—but justice, mercy, and kindness they forget. They would strain a gnat out of their soup and swallow a camel whole!" The disciples had to smile at the way Jesus put it. "They cannot understand what we are saying. We offend them—and when you offend men who take their religion very seriously, you must be ready for real trouble!"

The next Sabbath Day the disciples realized that the Pharisees were not going to stand by while Jesus taught the people a new way of life. Jesus had traveled to a small town near Capernaum where he had not been before and so he was invited to speak in the synagogue. Several Pharisees were present and very much interested in what Jesus said. They seemed friendly, and after the service went walking with Jesus and a few other people who clustered around Jesus. The group passed through a field of grain outside the town. James and Levi were hungry, so they pulled the tops off some wheatstalks. They rubbed the heads of wheat in their hands and blew away the chaff. The Pharisees seemed offended by this, but at first they said nothing. Other people saw what the disciples were doing, and they plucked wheat too. The Pharisees became more and more disturbed and finally could keep back their protests no longer. They came to Jesus.

"Rabbi, we noticed that some of the men here were pulling wheat," one of them said tactfully.

Jesus said: "They are hungry. It is all right for them to pick wheat, isn't it?"

"The scribes say it is all right to pick single grains, Rabbi," they replied, "but these men are rubbing out whole stalks, and that is against the Sabbath rule." They were sure that Jesus understood.

"Have you not read in the Bible that David and his warriors took bread off the sacred table in the Tabernacle when they were hungry?" asked Jesus. "That was against the rule of Moses —but David did it!"

The Pharisees were dumfounded. The first almost stammered as he asked, "What do you mean?"

"I mean that if there was a higher law for David there may also be a higher law for me and my disciples," answered Jesus plainly.

"But . . . but we do not understand," faltered the Pharisee. "You cannot set aside a law. No one can. That is impossible. It is part of our religion. Whoever pays no attention to the Law is an outcast and a sinner."

"The Sabbath was made for man, not man for the Sabbath,"

replied Jesus. "The Son of Man is lord of the Sabbath."

The older Pharisee frowned and then flushed red. The muscles in his neck tightened as he looked at Jesus. "You dare to say such things!" he burst out. "You do not belong to us. You are an enemy of God!"

All the way back to Capernaum the disciples talked about what had happened in the wheat field. "They just keep watching us to see if we do anything wrong!" protested James.

"Personally, I don't think they even understand what we are doing," ventured Andrew. "They never listen to what we say. They act as though they knew everything about religion."

"Yes, their kind of religion," remarked James indignantly. "They won't even speak to a leper! Who is going to go out among the people of our towns and let them know that God cares for them? Their religion is just for themselves!"

"Jesus is the only one who cares about the outcasts," said Simon earnestly. "No one else does."

Symeon hoped that Jesus would do something that would prove to everyone that he did not believe in God. The thought that Jesus might win the people over to himself struck panic into Symeon's heart. If that should happen, something desperate might have to be done. Meanwhile, however, he and a few others who knew how dangerous Jesus was had decided to wait.

On the next Sabbath Day, the whole matter came out into the open. As usual, most of the Jews in Capernaum—common people and Pharisees, along with Jesus and the disciples—came to the synagogue at the hour of worship. The moment Simon and Andrew entered they saw that there would be trouble: there was a man present with an arm made lame from dropsy—and they knew Jesus would surely heal him if he asked. The synagogue was crowded. The people bowed respectfully as Symeon and the leading men of the town entered, but they smiled when they had passed: Jesus was there, and they too had seen the man with the lame arm.

"Do you think he would dare to heal him?" one of the Pharisees whispered to Symeon.

"I hardly believe he will," replied Symeon. "To break the Sabbath law right in the synagogue would be a direct attack on religion."

At that moment the lame man went to where Jesus sat. Instantly the room was quiet. Everyone knew the charge against Jesus: that he broke the Law of God deliberately.

Jesus looked at the man and said, "Will you come with me?" He led the man to the front of the synagogue where he could speak to the elders and Pharisees.

"I ask you," demanded Jesus, "is it right to help or to hurt on the Sabbath Day? Should one save a life?" The men said nothing.

"Is there a single one of you that would leave a sheep in a ditch all day long if it fell in on Sabbath morning?" Everyone knew the rule: A farmer was permitted to save a sheep on the Sabbath.

"Well, isn't a man worth more than a sheep?"

The question was clear to every listener: Which was more important, the Sabbath rule or this man's need? Simon smiled, but the Pharisees felt differently. Symeon could hardly contain himself. He wanted to rise up and cry out to everyone that these were trick questions; that this bold Nazarene was trying to tear down the sacred Law of God himself; that religion itself would be destroyed if he succeeded. But he sat still and said nothing.

Jesus turned to the man. "Stretch out your arm," he said gently.

The instant the man obeyed, his withered arm became as strong as the other. A murmur of awe went over the congregation. Symeon rose and strode out of the synagogue, followed by the religious officials of Capernaum. Outside, Symeon turned to the others and declared firmly: "We must save our holy religion at all costs. He has won over the people with his trickery, but God is on our side! We must go to King Herod and ask him to help us put this man out of the way!"

7. MISSIONARIES OF THE KINGDOM

IT TOOK less than a week for the report that Jesus had defied the
Pharisees to spread throughout all Galilee. Those who most
welcomed the news were the Zealots. For a long time, they had
been plotting to rebel against the Romans, but so far had found
no plan that promised to be successful. They believed that Jesus
was the leader for whom they had been waiting so long. He was
brave. He stood up to the officials. He was popular with the common people. One of their leaders decided to find out what Jesus
intended to do. His name was Simon. Well known in Galilee for
his courage, everyone called him "the Zealot." He made a special
trip to Capernaum that same week and came to Simon's home.
Before the week was past he became a follower of Jesus. But there
were many things he found it hard to understand.

"Tell me," he asked Simon and James privately, "does the
Rabbi intend to set up the new kingdom now?"

Simon was cautious. "The Master has said nothing about that."

The Zealot glanced about to make sure that the door and shutters were tightly closed. "Do you not know that he could easily
persuade the people to revolt against Herod?"

James was alarmed. "But we're not ready for that yet."

Simon gave him a warning glance. He still mistrusted this man. "We plan to tell everyone in this country our message," he said guardedly.

"If you are going to establish a free Jewish nation, you must do more than talk," declared the Zealot. "You should organize!"

The fishermen looked at each other, doubting how much they should say. Finally James said vaguely, "We think it won't be much longer."

"Why can't we do something definite about it?" said the Zealot.

"Do you really think he could be king of the Jews?" asked James.

"I'm certain of it!" replied the Zealot. "My people would follow him to a man!"

James looked inquiringly at Simon. "I think most of the people would be favorable, don't you?"

Simon shook his head doubtfully. "We ought to see what the Master thinks. King Herod has many Roman soldiers under his command!"

"Listen, Simon," argued James. "The Master has spent plenty of time teaching already. Everyone in Galilee has heard about the kingdom." Simon didn't reply. "He intends to fight eventually," continued James. "Didn't he say he came to bring conflict and not peace? I think it is about time to stop talking and get to work!"

Simon stared at the ground. "Well, one thing is sure," he admitted. "The Pharisees are all against us. They will keep us out of the synagogues."

"That is exactly why I think Jesus should openly declare himself king," affirmed the Zealot strongly. "It is time to go forward!"

Jesus had told the disciples to wait for him in Capernaum and had gone to the hills for prayer. He knew his work had reached a turning point. For several days he remained alone, praying and seeking wisdom from God. When he returned to Capernaum, he called the disciples together.

"My followers," he said gravely, when they were gathered about him, "many times I have told you that the Kingdom of

God cannot come without suffering. Men who hate truth hate anyone who speaks the truth." The men knew Jesus had made a decision. "The Kingdom of God has been proclaimed only in Galilee," he continued. "The time has now come to carry the news to all Palestine!"

That means Judea! thought James and John at the same time. In Jerusalem the priests and Pharisees were strongest.

"Rulers will show us no mercy," said Jesus. "God is our only Source of strength. We must tell the gospel in every village and countryside. We must not miss a single Jew. You are to be my missionaries to this nation!"

The men stirred and glanced at one another. The Zealot vigorously nodded his approval. No hiding in the hills for them; they were going forward! Fear mixed with eagerness sent chills through them.

Jesus rose and stood facing Simon, who went to his knees before him. Jesus laid his hand on Simon's head and, lifting up his eyes, prayed for him. He asked the Heavenly Father to strengthen him and to give him the wisdom and courage he would need for the important task he was about to undertake. One by one, Jesus blessed each of the twelve men. He knew them better than they knew themselves and he prayed simply and frankly for each one. Awe filled them as they listened. The work was so great, and they were so weak! They were to teach and heal as Jesus himself had been doing! A new spirit gripped them.

"Shall we too be able to drive out demons and raise the dead, Master?" asked Simon.

"The power of the Kingdom is yours," declared Jesus. "You have both the right and the power to destroy evil wherever you find it—whether demons, sickness, or spiritual blindness."

Then he gave them instructions for the journey that lay before them. "You are to travel two by two. Preach only to Jews, not to Samaritans or gentiles, for the time is short. Your work is to seek everywhere the lost sheep of the people of Israel. Return when this is done.

"Take only a walking stick and one pair of sandals—neither food nor money nor extra clothes."

"How shall we live, Master? Where shall we stay?" asked Simon.

"When you come to a strange town, find someone who will open his home to you while you work there," answered Jesus. "Once you have decided with whom you will stay, do not change. Hold fast to your first friend."

"What if no one will take us in?" asked Andrew.

"If you find no one who will help you, leave that town immediately," answered Jesus. "God will judge any town that will not hear your message.

"This is your gospel: Tell all Jews that God has come among us. Tell them that his power is right now at work. Tell them that he is the ruler of all who trust him. Warn them to repent and turn to him now." The disciples realized that they would have to face the people without Jesus.

"I am sending you out like sheep among wolves," warned Jesus. "You will be persecuted. Never put your trust in persons in high positions, for they will betray you.

"If you are put in prison and brought into court, do not be anxious about what you should say. The spirit of God your Father will help you, and everyone who hears you will learn the good news that God's Kingdom has come."

"Master, how shall we ever have strength to do it?" burst out Andrew.

"Do not be afraid!" Jesus was standing now, ready to bid them farewell. "God has given you his own power. You carry news of eternal life; you are doing the work of God's Kingdom!"

A few days later, one of the Twelve visited Nazareth. He saw the mother and brothers of Jesus and told them how Jesus was sending missionaries of the Kingdom to every village in Palestine. Mary was at once fearful.

"That will put him in great danger," she said nervously.

"He has already made a big enough fool of himself," remarked one of her sons rudely. He was a strong young fellow about twenty-five. "The trouble with him is that people make too much of him."

"Don't speak that way, Jude," protested Mary. She had spent many sleepless nights wondering if the rumor could be true that

Jesus had become a fanatic and was not in his right mind.

"Bah! The only trouble with him is that popularity has gone to his head!"

"What should I do, Jude?" asked Mary. "He is bound to get into some kind of trouble if he goes on like this."

"Oh, I don't know." Jude wished his mother would stop worrying. "Perhaps we can make him come home."

Mary snatched at the suggestion. "Let us go to him right away." She prepared hastily for the trip, greatly relieved to be doing something about her strange son Jesus.

Upon arriving at Capernaum, Mary and Jude went directly to the home of Simon where they knew Jesus stayed. They found the courtyard crowded. Mary was dismayed.

"Don't worry," said Jude. "He will come when I tell him you are here waiting for him." He began to shove through the tightly packed people. There were angry murmurs, but Jude paid no attention. As he got farther into the courtyard he could hear a man shouting angrily. *That's not Jesus' voice,* he thought. Finally he reached a place where he could see his brother.

Behind Jesus stood some of the disciples who had already returned from their mission. All around him were sick and lame people, but he was not healing them. He was standing silently before the man whose harsh voice Jude had heard. The man was completely out of control of himself. Jude couldn't see why he was so angry, but he thought this must have been going on for some time.

"Who is the angry one?" he asked a bystander.

"Some scribe."

The scribe had almost run out of breath, but Jesus still said nothing. Irritated by Jesus' silence, he threw a final accusation at him.

"You false prophet! You are a complete fake!"

A man in the crowd suddenly cried out: "He is not false! He tells us the truth as no man ever did."

"He has brought healing to many," added another. "How could he do that if he were not sent from God?" Others nodded.

The angry scribe turned on the man. "Many magicians can heal and drive out demons! I can show you a hundred right here in Galilee who can do anything he can! Bah! This prophet of yours is a fake!"

The man did not know what to answer. "I'll tell you why he can drive out demons," snapped the enraged scribe. "I'll tell you! The prince of all demons has got hold of him! That's why he can do it!" Scornfully he drove home his point. "Why shouldn't he be stronger than the demons? He is possessed by Satan himself."

Simon flushed. The charge was crude and ridiculous. He opened his mouth to deny it, but he realized he could not. How could he prove the scribe wrong? Simon's anger turned to shame.

Jesus' voice was calm and controlled, when at last he spoke. "Would Satan cast out his own helpers?" he asked the man, coolly. There was a touch of sarcasm in his voice. "A nation divided within itself will fall! Has Satan risen up against himself and given me power to destroy his own power over men?"

Jude was amazed at the power of his brother's words. This did not sound as though he were out of his mind!

Jesus did not give the scribe a chance to reply. "No!" he declared, speaking now to all the people. "I have no demon. No one can enter a man's house and take his property without first binding the owner with ropes. I have power to cast out demons because I have overcome the prince of all evil!"

The answer could not be denied. Looking sternly at the scribe, Jesus said: "I tell you, men will be forgiven all their sins and blasphemies except one: If you harden yourself against the Holy Spirit, you commit eternal sin!" Jesus then raised his voice. "By the very finger of God I cast out demons—and because I have overcome the evil one himself, God is now ruling among you!"

An excited woman cried out, "How fortunate your mother is to have such a son!"

"The person who is truly fortunate is the one who hears and believes the Word of God," answered Jesus quickly.

Jude looked at the woman startled. She had said his mother was fortunate—but to Mary Jesus was a great worry! Remembering why he had come, Jude began to push his way toward

Jesus. When finally he could get no farther, he touched the shoulder of a man ahead of him. "Would you tell the Rabbi that his mother and brothers want to see him outside?"

When the man delivered the message to Jesus, the disciples stepped forward and started to clear a path, but Jesus put out his hand and stopped them. He looked around at the faces of the loyal men who had left everything to follow him and at the sick and anxious people sitting on the hard-packed dirt of the courtyard.

"Who is my mother, and who are my brothers?" The words were gentle, very different from his tone a moment before. "I tell you, you are my mother and my brothers! Anyone who does the will of God is my brother, my sister, my mother!

"A true missionary of the Kingdom must be willing to give up his own family for my sake and take the people of God's Kingdom for his family. Anyone who thinks more of his own mother, wife, or child, than he does of the Kingdom cannot be my disciple."

"Master, we have given up everything to follow you," said Simon.

"You may have to give even your life, Simon," answered Jesus. "Yet great is your reward in heaven."

Jude pushed his way out of the courtyard. The first thing he said to his mother was, "Jesus seems like another person."

Despair darkened Mary's expression. "Do you mean that what the people are saying about him is true?" she asked.

"No, no. I didn't mean that," Jude said quickly. "He is different in another way. He is . . . he is not like us any more." He tried to describe Jesus but could not.

"Well, what happened?" Mary was relieved but puzzled. "What did he do?" Jude then told her all that he had seen from the moment he had entered the courtyard. She listened, wondering at the son who had left her home only a few months before. When Jude finished she turned to leave.

"Wait, mother!" said Jude. "Don't you want to see him?"

"There is no reason for us to see him, my son," replied Mary quietly. "He doesn't need us to care for him. This is God's work that he is doing." That same day Mary returned to Naz-areth, filled with wonder at the things that had happened.

Not only Mary but the disciples too were amazed at Jesus' power. Even the Zealot, the most eager to start spreading the news of the Kingdom, saw how much he needed to learn before attempting to do Jesus' work. At the table that evening, Simon spoke the feeling of them all.

"Master, how shall we ever be strong enough to be your missionaries?"

"Whoever knows God, lives by his power, Simon," answered Jesus. "The evil one does not rule such men."

"But I believe in God, Master," said Simon. "Yet I cannot heal anyone." He paused and then added in a tone of despair, "I could never have answered that scribe!"

"Simon, if you had real faith in God—even a tiny grain—you would be able to do great things."

"I have prayed many times and still I do not have the strength," said Simon humbly.

"Listen to me," said Jesus. "Suppose you were to go to a friend's house late at night and say: 'Friend, will you lend me three loaves of bread? A visitor has arrived unexpectedly and I am out of food.' Suppose he were to answer: 'Don't bother me. I'm in bed and the door is locked. I can't get up.' What would you do?"

After a pause, John answered, "Why, you just keep on knock-ing until he *does* get up!" The disciples smiled.

"True!" said Jesus. "He may not get up because of friendli-ness, but if you keep on knocking, he'll give you the bread just to get rid of you! But God is your friend! Will he not give you what you ask? But you must not grow weary in asking.

"In a certain town," he continued, "there was a very unfair judge. He didn't care about anyone. There was a poor widow in that town who was being mistreated. Again and again she went to the judge and asked him to help her—but he never paid any attention. Finally he said to himself: 'I don't care about this woman, but she is becoming a nuisance. Perhaps if I give her what she wants she will stop pestering me.'" Jesus said very emphatically, "If this wicked man finally helped a widow because she kept on asking for justice, won't God, who is good and just, answer you if you pray sincerely?"

Simon saw how little real faith he had in spite of all his praying. How often he had thought to himself, *Now I'll pray and see what happens.* He had been testing God, not trusting him!

"O Master," he urged, "won't you teach us to pray as John the Baptizer taught his disciples?"

"When you pray, say: 'Our Father in heaven, holy be thy name. Thy Kingdom come, thy will be done on earth as it is in heaven.' "

Most of the time, the disciples had to admit, they thought only of persuading God to do what they wanted.

"Ask your Heavenly Father, 'Give us today the food we will need to do our work tomorrow,' " said Jesus. "Anyone who serves God trusts him for all things he needs day by day.

"Then you must ask God to forgive you your sins. But if you are not willing to forgive others, do not think for one moment that God will forgive you."

"Master, how often shall someone sin against me and I go on forgiving him?" asked Peter. "Seven times?"

'Not seven times, Peter, but seventy times seven." Jesus paused and then went on. "The Kingdom of Heaven is like a king who decided to settle his accounts with his servants. The king ordered one man, with his wife and children, to be sold into slavery, and all his possessions sold for cash so that the debt could be met.

"The servant fell on his knees and begged, 'Master have patience with me and I will pay you every penny.' Out of pity, the king released him and forgave him the whole debt.

"On his way home, the servant met a fellow servant who owed him a very small sum of money. He grabbed the poor fellow by the throat and demanded, 'You pay me what you owe me!' The man fell on his knees and begged, 'Have patience with me and I will pay you.' But he refused. Instead, he put him into prison until the debt should be paid. The other servants saw how unfair this was and they told the king what had happened.

"The king called for the unjust servant and said: 'You wicked servant! When you asked, I forgave you all that you owed me—should you not have been merciful to your fellow servant, as I was merciful to you?' Very angry, the king threw the unjust man into jail to remain there until his whole debt was paid.

"Neither can you be forgiven," concluded Jesus, "unless you forgive others from your heart."

After a moment John said: "Do you really think God pays attention to us, Master? He seems so far away. Oh, I know he watches over the nation—but I am not sure he cares what happens to me!"

Jesus nodded toward Simon. "Simon loves his children," he said. "Simon, if your little son should ask you for a piece of bread, would you give him a rock to eat? Or if he asked for a broiled fish, would you give him a poisonous snake instead? Or if he asked for an egg, would you give him a scorpion with a deadly stinger?"

"No, of course not!" exclaimed Simon.

"Well, then, if you can do that much for your children, do you not think that God will do far more for those who trust him?"

Jesus lifted his arms to pray. It seemed to Simon that Jesus was praying specially for him when he asked the Heavenly Father to send the Holy Spirit upon them all. As they left the place of prayer, Simon and Andrew dropped behind the others.

"What I cannot understand," said Andrew, "is how he knows all these things. Where did he learn it all?"

"It is strange," agreed Simon. "You would almost think he came down from heaven, wouldn't you?"

8. HE IS MORE THAN A TEACHER

FAR away to the south, John the Baptizer was imprisoned in King Herod's fortress at Machaerus. Through the bars of his tiny window he could see the green waters of the Dead Sea far below and the rocky hills of Judea beyond. He did not expect to lie in this dungeon long. At any moment the Day of Judgment might come; God would send hosts of angels to punish wrongdoers and to reward his faithful servants.

John listened intently to the news that his followers brought about Jesus. They told him all that Jesus did: his demand that all men should repent; the new teaching about the Kingdom of God which was the talk of men everywhere. John was amazed at the power Jesus had to heal many sick people; he was glad when he heard that Jesus was not afraid of the Pharisees.

But as days passed, doubts began to creep into the Baptizer's mind. Could God have chosen this man to deliver His people? John could not understand why the deliverance did not come. Jesus was training only a handful of disciples to preach. It would

take more than that to bring God's great day. At last the Prophet
sent two messengers to Jesus.

"Our Prophet, John the Baptizer, has sent us to ask a question," said the leader. "Are you the One whom God has sent to
judge the wicked and justify the faithful?"

This very question was stirring in the minds of the disciples.
Why did Jesus not tell them plainly who he was?

"Are you the Messiah of God?" repeated the man. "Or should
we look for someone else?"

"You know what I teach," answered Jesus. "You have heard
about the things that I do. Go back to John and tell him that
the eyes of the blind are opened; the lame walk; lepers are
cleansed—the good news that God is present among men is declared to everyone who will listen."

"But, Rabbi," said the puzzled leader, "what shall we tell the
Prophet? Are you truly the Messiah?"

"How do you expect to know the Messiah?" asked Jesus.
"What will he do that you will recognize him?" The men did
not answer. "Isaiah the Prophet said: 'Here is my servant, my
Chosen One. He will not be loud and noisy: He will not raise a
great shout in public. He will not break a bent sapling or even
blow out the tiniest lamp flame!' "

The followers of John murmured to themselves. "The Messiah—coming silently? . . . You say he won't even break a twig?"
The ideas seemed to escape them, slipping away as soon as they
were spoken.

Andrew was distressed at Jesus' words. "Master, the Messiah
is mighty! He will come from the sky in great glory. How can
you say that the Messiah will come without people even knowing
he is among us?"

Jesus turned to the followers of John the Baptizer and said:
"Go tell John what you have heard. He truly knows the will of
God if he understands these things I have said."

Impulsively Andrew reached out his hand to stop the men.
But then he drew back: *Jesus had told them to go.* He turned to
Jesus the instant they left and demanded, "How *does* the Mes-
siah come?"

"Andrew," replied Jesus patiently, "don't you understand yet what I mean when I tell you that the Kingdom of God is at hand?"

Andrew could not hide his disappointment. Jesus knew how hard it was for his disciple to grasp what he meant. Hopes that he had held for years were not easy to give up quickly.

"Then John the Baptizer was wrong?" Andrew's voice was subdued. "The Messiah will not come with an army of angels to destroy the enemies of his people?"

Jesus answered gently. "Among all men, none is greater than John. He was sent to prepare the way for me. Just the same, the very least person in the Kingdom is greater than John."

Andrew sighed. He could not believe Jesus was wrong. And yet it was hard to be satisfied with a kingdom that did not set the people free from oppression, even if it was a kingdom of truth and help for the poor.

"You will soon be sent out to spread the news of the true Kingdom through this land," said Jesus. "You must find out for yourselves how great is the power God has sent among you."

During the week that followed, Jesus led the twelve men through the country on the other side of the Lake of Galilee. The power of his words and actions amazed his disciples. Not until the day they returned to Galilee, however, did the disciples begin to grasp for themselves the true meaning of what was happening.

While Jesus was absent from Capernaum with the Twelve, disease struck down the daughter of a man named Jairus, an elder of the synagogue. Jairus had strongly disapproved when the high priest ordered the elders of his synagogue to forbid Jesus to preach there, but he had been unable to do anything about it.

The doctors in Capernaum could not help the girl. Jairus was terribly worried. Then he thought of Jesus. Perhaps this great Teacher could heal his daughter! His heart sank when Simon's wife told him that Jesus and the others were in the country of Gadara, across the lake, and that she did not know when they would be back.

Every minute that Jairus did not spend at the bedside of the sick child, he watched the lake for a sign of Jesus' return. Three nights he sat up with his little girl. As he hastened anxiously to the shore of the lake on the last morning, he said sadly to himself, "If the Rabbi does not come today, I shall never see my child alive again."

Near the lake he caught sight of a crowd of people on the shore and broke into a run.

Jesus had just stepped out of the boat. Jairus pushed into the crowd, thinking only of his dying daughter. He knelt imploringly at Jesus' feet.

"O Rabbi! Help me! I am in great trouble!"

The disciples looked at one another in mild surprise. Was not this one of the elders of the synagogue?

"These fellows are much humbler when they want something," remarked Andrew to John.

"I know what I'd do if I were in the Master's place," murmured John.

Jesus instantly sensed the desperate worry that had driven every other thought from Jairus' mind. "What is it you need?" The disciples felt that the very tone of Jesus' voice was a rebuke to their vengeful feelings.

"My little daughter," said Jairus, brokenly. "At this very moment she is dying. Please come and pray for her, that she may live, and not die!"

"We must hurry," said Jesus and started swiftly toward Capernaum. The people followed closely. The disciples hurried to keep up with Jesus, but he paid no attention to them. The anxious father stayed close beside Jesus.

Suddenly Jesus stopped. "Hurry, Rabbi," begged Jairus earnestly. "She may not live much longer." But Jesus seemed not to hear. He looked at the disciples, who were wondering why he had stopped.

"Who touched me?" Jesus turned around where he stood.

Simon laughed shortly and said: "What do you mean, Master? In a crowd like this, a dozen people could have touched you!"

"Just the same, I felt someone." Jesus searched the crowd behind Simon. Most of the people looked at him blankly. Jesus continued to scan the crowd. Even Jairus held back his urgent protest to hasten.

At that moment there was a disturbance in the crowd, and a trembling woman came up to Jesus. "I touched you, Rabbi," she confessed tearfully.

Jesus said to her kindly, "Why did you do it?"

"Rabbi, I have been sick for twelve years. I have spent all my money on doctors and I am worse than ever."

"Why did you touch me?" asked Jesus.

"I thought, *If I can touch only the edge of his robe, I shall be healed.*" Then very simply she added. "So I did, Rabbi—and now I am well!"

"It is your faith in God that has healed you," said Jesus to the kneeling woman. "Do not tremble and be afraid. It is faith like yours that God most desires."

While Jesus was speaking, a man had hurried down the street toward them. Jairus recognized one of his own servants. "Hurry, Master! Oh, hurry!" he cried. But he knew it was too late.

The servant came to him sadly. "She is dead. There is no use bothering the Rabbi any more."

Jesus turned to Jairus. "Courage, sir! Do not be sorrowful."

"What a shame!" Simon remembered his own children and knew how the man felt. "His little one is dead!"

Jesus turned to the disciples and said, "You saw a woman healed through faith." They looked at him, wondering what he meant. To Jairus, Jesus said, "Come, take me to your home." All hope was gone for Jairus, but obediently he led the way.

Already the hired wailers filled Jairus' house. Their loud cries of grief, the shrill sound of flutes playing funeral music, and the hysterical weeping of the friends of the child's mother made such noise that Jesus could hardly be heard.

"Why all this wailing?" Jesus cried. The noise quieted a little. "The child is not dead! She is only asleep!"

The wailers burst into derisive laughter. "She sleeps soundly!"

"Clear this crowd out of here," Jesus commanded. Jairus was glad to be rid of them. Amid angry murmurs, he sent every single one of them out of the house.

Several of the disciples were waiting outside; they watched the hired wailers leave. "What do you suppose is going on?"

asked Andrew. They waited a little longer, but at last the suspense was too much.

"Come on," said the Zealot, "let's go in." They pressed through the front door into an empty room. "Where have they gone?" The sound of soft weeping came from the next room. Hesitating now, they went nearer so that they could look through a doorway. The men never forgot what they saw.

The little girl was standing beside the bed looking up at Jesus. He held her hand in his. Her mother had thrown her arms around Jairus and was weeping. Simon, James, and John stood speechless, staring at the child who a moment before had been lying dead.

"She is alive!" gasped Andrew. The child turned toward them, but the disciples shrank back as though fearful of what they saw.

"I'm hungry," she said.

Jesus gripped Jairus' shoulder gently. "Give the child something to eat now." Neither of the parents replied; but they kneeled before Jesus.

The awed disciples turned toward Jesus. Could this man who gave life to the dead be the Master they knew so well?

"For your sakes," Jesus said, "I am glad I was not here when this child died." His words struck deep into the memories of the disciples. "I have come to tell you what life really is. This child was dead and lives again. But I warn you: there is a kind of death from which no one can return. And there is true life: whoever has this life can never die."

Who is he—who is this One who raises the dead? The minds of the disciples raced, trying to grasp the meaning of what had happened.

"Fear not the death of the body; he who believes in God can never die. Just as I have given life to this little child I give eternal life to all who put their trust in God."

Who can he be—who can he be—to give eternal life?

Jesus turned to the parents of the child. "Rise!" Then he warned them and the disciples, saying: "No one must hear about this. Only you understand its true meaning." Turning to the disciples, he said, "Let us go now." Seething with excitement they could not control, the disciples followed Jesus.

9. HOW WILL YOU KNOW
THE MESSIAH?

ONE week later a messenger arrived at the court of King Herod, in Tiberias, a city not far from Capernaum on the Lake of Galilee. He carried reports from local officials throughout the provinces that Herod ruled. As he read them, the king became more and more alarmed. Finally he turned to a slave. "Tell my officers to come immediately!"

When the high officials of the court arrived, Herod waved the papers and said, "Every single governor reports that there are Jews going through our cities and towns talking about some new kingdom!" He looked at them sharply. "Do you know anything about this?"

After a moment one of them answered, "There is a carpenter from Nazareth preaching something like that."

"Do you think he has anything to do with this business?"

"I am not sure," answered the man. "I know a Pharisee in Capernaum who says this fellow wants to do away with the Jewish religion." The man speaking was one of the Herodians whom Symeon had stirred up against Jesus.

"What sort of man is he?" demanded Herod.

"He has great influence with the people," he said. "This Pharisee admits that his miracles are not tricks."

"Miracles!" Herod became very sober. "Who is this man?" he demanded. "Has John the Baptizer risen from the dead?" Against his better judgment he had executed the Prophet a few weeks before.

"That is not possible," answered an officer.

"We shall have a revolution on our hands if this really is John." Herod turned to the officer who had spoken last. "Who is he, if he isn't John?"

"People say different things. Some say he is Elijah; others say someone else, but they all think he is a prophet."

"That is exactly what they said about John the Baptizer," exclaimed Herod.

"John never sent out missionaries!" objected the Herodian.

"That only makes it worse!" The king pointed to the reports in front of him. "What if these Jews are working for him?"

"They might be," admitted the man.

If Herod could have heard the conversation of Simon and Andrew at that moment, he would have been even more anxious. They were in high spirits as they walked the last mile of their trip back to Capernaum.

"How glad everyone has been to hear about the Kingdom!" remarked Simon. "Do you not think that these people are ready to make the Master their king?"

"They are very discontented," agreed Andrew. "Herod has crushed them so that they are ready to do about anything."

For a distance they walked in silence. Finally Simon said: "I cannot understand what it is about the Master. Even evil spirits seem to fear him!"

"Do you suppose this trip has made the others feel the way we do?" wondered Andrew.

When Simon and Andrew arrived in Capernaum, they found that James, John, and the Zealot had returned ahead of them. They were telling Jesus about their experiences.

"The evil spirits themselves obeyed us in your name!" exclaimed John.

"You have good reason to rejoice," answered Jesus. "Nevertheless, you should rejoice because you have done the will of God—not because you have conquered evil spirits."

"Well, Master," remarked the Zealot practically, "not everyone was glad to see us. I had trouble with the Pharisees. They just argue and argue."

"We talked to them too," said Andrew. He was troubled. "Many times we tried to tell them the news of the eternal Kingdom, but they would never receive what we said."

"Do you remember the story of the Sower, Andrew?" asked Jesus.

"I never understood what you meant, Master," answered Andrew.

"Listen carefully. The farmer who went out to sow was planting the seed of eternal life. Some fell on the road at the edge of the field, and the birds ate it up. This is like the person who hears my word but immediately forgets because Satan robs him of it.

"Some of the seed fell on stony soil. It grew fast, but when the hot sun shone it withered away because it had weak roots. This is like the person who is very enthusiastic at first, but as soon as he has to work or suffer, he gives up.

"Other seed fell among weeds, which kept it from growing strong. This is like the person who hears the word but is so worried or busy trying to get ahead of other people that he forgets all about God.

"But then there is the seed that fell on good soil; it grew deep roots and produced a fine harvest. This is like the person who hears and really understands my words. He knows what eternal life is, and helps other people to find it."

"Do you know," the Zealot broke in, "I should not be surprised if some of the Pharisees would join us when we show our strength!"

"My Kingdom is not of this world," answered Jesus. "No one who is seeking political power will join us. Only persons who want to do the will of God belong in my Kingdom."

"But, Master," responded the Zealot, "almost everyone listened eagerly to us! It will not be difficult to start the Kingdom in Galilee!"

"We probably could unite the Jews against Herod," replied Jesus, "but that is not our business. God sent me into the world to proclaim the news of an eternal Kingdom!"

Simon turned to the Zealot. "You seem to think the people listened only because they hope we will free them from the Romans. I do not doubt that they would be glad to be rid of the Romans; but from what I saw, I think they listened because we told them about the rule of God!"

"Isn't that the same thing?" retorted the Zealot.

Jesus saw that most of the disciples still did not understand clearly what he was trying to do. But he had little opportunity to explain further, because the people of Capernaum were every day crowding to the home of Simon. When all of the Twelve had at last returned from their mission, he said to them, "Let us cross the lake and find a quiet place where we can rest and talk."

They hoped to leave unseen, but many people followed them down to the lake where Simon's boat was.

"Don't you see what I mean?" exclaimed the Zealot. "What a wonderful chance we have to lead them against Herod!"

"Let us go over toward Bethsaida," replied Jesus. "I know a hill where very few people pass by." James and John turned the boat toward the hills nearly three miles across the lake.

The disappointed people watched Jesus and the disciples push off. A few men left the group and began to walk along the shore. Soon the others realized that they were going to go on foot around the lake. Some walked, but others ran.

"I believe the whole crowd is going to follow us," remarked Andrew, looking back.

"They are like sheep without a shepherd," remarked Jesus.

By the time the disciples had rowed across the lake, the people were beginning to arrive. "I think I know a place where we can get away from them," said Philip. He had lived in this part of the country.

"We cannot send them away, Philip," answered Jesus. When the boat landed he led the crowd to a grassy spot on the hillside overlooking the lake below.

All afternoon Jesus taught them. When at last the sun touched the hills of Galilee across the lake, the disciples interrupted.

"Master," they said, "don't you think we had better send them away before it gets dark?"

"It is late," added Philip, "and there is no place to buy food here. They will need to go to the villages."

"That isn't necessary, is it?" said Jesus. "*You* give them something to eat."

The disciples looked at him blankly. "We didn't bring any provisions with us, Master," said James. "And besides, even if we had, it would never be enough to feed this crowd!"

Jesus turned to Philip. "What shall we do, Philip?"

"Master, even if there were a town near here, it would take far more money than we have to buy enough food to give each person a tiny bit!"

"How many loaves have we all together?" asked Jesus.

The disciples found, as they expected, that the people had brought no food. "This seems foolish to me," remarked James. Finally Andrew found a boy with some loaves and fish. The boy let Andrew take the lunch to Jesus.

"Tell the people to sit down in groups," said Jesus. Before them all he held one of the loaves in his hands and thanked God for it; then he broke it in pieces. "Distribute this among the people," he instructed the disciples.

"This boy's loaves and fish will satisfy your hunger now," said Jesus to the eager crowd. "If you eat only this kind of food, you will eventually die. I have another kind to give you: if you will eat the Bread of eternal life, you will never die!

"Come and eat this Bread—you will never hunger again. You must hear and believe my word, for the Father in heaven has sent me to you."

While the people ate, they whispered among themselves in amazement. Where had this food come from? They could hardly believe what the people near Jesus said: that he had broken the loaves and fish again and again, until everyone had enough.

The Zealot turned to James. "They will do anything for a person who gives them food," he said.

Jesus knew the people were thinking how good it was to receive the food. "God sent manna to your ancestors while they were in the desert," he cried out, "but they died. The true Bread from heaven gives you eternal life. Eat this Bread and you shall never hunger again!"

"Give us this Bread!" called out a man in the crowd. "We do not want to be hungry any more."

"Do not follow me because I give you loaves and fish—that kind of food perishes," replied Jesus. "Rather, believe my word, in order that you may have eternal life!"

But the people could think only of the free food Jesus had given them. They paid no attention to his words. "We will do anything for you!" they cried. Then another shout grew loud.

"You shall be our king! You shall be our king!"

"They are going to compel him to be king!" exclaimed the Zealot.

Jesus turned his back and called his disciples about him.

"What is he going to do?" The Zealot was alarmed. "Surely he won't miss this opportunity?"

"Let us go," said Jesus to the Twelve, starting toward the lake shore.

The Zealot caught Jesus' arm. "But, Master . . ." He let go as Simon gripped his shoulder.

"He will be king all right," Simon told him. "But he is not the kind of king these people want. I am sure of that."

The crowd were dumfounded to see Jesus leave them so quickly. A few attempted to follow, but they soon realized that twilight was swiftly fading into the darkness of night and they turned back.

"You row across to Capernaum by yourselves," said Jesus to the disciples. "I will follow later." The wondering men got into the boat and rowed away. Jesus stood watching them as they disappeared in the deep twilight. Then he turned and walked alone into the shadowy hills.

"Sometimes I wonder if he knows what he is doing!" burst out the Zealot, bitterly disappointed. "What an opportunity! He just turned his back on them!"

"You know he has no desire for political power," said John.

"How can we ever establish the government of God if we never do anything practical?" asked the Zealot. "What will his teachings ever amount to unless we put them in the place of the old laws?"

Simon could not forget the words of Jesus. "He did not say, 'I am your King.' He said, 'I am the Bread of Life.' "

"What do you mean?" asked the Zealot.

"Are you sure he intends to start a rebellion?" asked Simon.

"I don't know what else all this talk of a Kingdom could mean!"

"If he were an ordinary political leader—or even a Rabbi— there would be no other way," said Simon, reflectively. "But there is something about him that makes me think he is not going to do what we expect at all!"

A gust of cold wind struck them, and the men looked up. Even the western sky was black. The boat was in the middle of the lake. Out of the dark night the wind blew in ever stronger gusts.

"We're in for a squall," said James, worried. The boat rolled. It was heavily loaded, and water splashed in.

"Steer into the waves," called Simon. James and John tried to pull the boat around, but the wind had caught them. The boat swung broadside and lurched dangerously in the trough of the waves. Water poured in. Simon stepped swiftly to the center and sat down beside James. Together they pulled the heavy oar; after a tense moment the boat swung slowly around.

"We've got to bail this water out," said Simon. More came over the side with each roll.

"If we don't get this water out, we'll never get to shore," shouted Simon.

"What can we do?" cried the Zealot. Waves continued to leap over the side into the boat. Desperately the men tried to bail out the water. "We'll never make it!" they cried, seized by panic.

Andrew clutched John's shoulder. "Look! What's that?" He pointed out into the blackness.

"It's a ghost!" screamed one of the Twelve. The men forgot the waves. Terror gripped them. "O Father in heaven," cried Simon, "save us!"

"Do not be afraid! It is I!"

Gradually it came to the men that it was the voice of Jesus they were hearing. "Oh, save us, Master!" Fear began to melt away. Jesus was in their midst.

"Why are you terrified?" he asked. "Have you no faith, even after being with me all this time?"

The white crest on the waves disappeared. The boat lay deep in the water, but danger was past. Almost afraid to look, the disciples turned to Jesus. Who could he be—that he had power to calm the storm?

"Did I not give life to the little child in Capernaum?" said Jesus. "Did I not give bread to the hungry crowds? Do you not yet understand?"

10. "YOU ARE THE CHRIST"

THE household of Symeon the Pharisee was stirring with excitement. During the day the servants had put the house in perfect order, and now the cooks were preparing a banquet for the evening. Symeon himself was trying to make up his mind whether he should wear his highly ornamented robe. Finally he decided against it and chose another with fine cloth but very few trimmings. A sensible Pharisee did not try to dress too elegantly when an important official was to be his guest.

The banquet table was beautiful. The servants had lighted candles to celebrate the victory of the great Jewish general, Judas Maccabaeus, who had driven foreign tyrants out of Palestine and purified the Temple two hundred years before. There was roast lamb, deliciously cooked, and all the best food which

Symeon could afford to set before his guest of honor. Nothing could be too good for a scribe sent by the highest authority of the Jewish religion, the high priest himself!

Not until late in the evening did Symeon's visitor arrive from his long journey. At dinner the men ate in dignified silence, but Symeon was burning with curiosity. The messenger who had brought news of the arrival of the scribe had told Symeon only that the high priest desired more information about certain things that were happening in Galilee. Symeon was sure that the matter concerned Jesus of Nazareth.

Only when he had finished the dinner did the scribe speak to Symeon. "You are a generous host, my friend."

Symeon smiled and bowed his head gratefully. The scribe settled himself comfortably. "I come on very delicate business. It must remain a secret." The servants came in to clear the table, and he stopped speaking. Then Symeon sent them out and closed the door. "The high priest tells me that you know this Jesus of Nazareth. Have you kept a close watch on him during the last few months?"

"Yes," replied Symeon, complimented by this confidential question. "I know all that he has done."

"As you remember, several months ago we ordered the elders of all the congregations to keep this Nazarene out of our synagogues," continued the scribe. "But of course that did not keep him from preaching to the people in public places." He looked keenly at Symeon. "Not a word of this must come to the common people!"

"Naturally," agreed Symeon.

"Very well, then," said the scribe. "Do you think that we can convince his followers that their Rabbi is not to be trusted?"

"That will be hard," answered Symeon. "He is more popular than ever." Then he told the scribe in detail how Jesus had fed the crowd of five thousand people.

"It sounds as though he might even have it in his power to persuade them to revolt," observed the scribe when Symeon had finished.

"They actually did try to make him their king!" exclaimed Symeon.

"Does Herod know about that?" asked the man.

"We have told some of the people at his court about it," replied Symeon. "If you want to know what I think—Herod is afraid to do anything! He thinks the Nazarene is John the Baptizer risen from the dead!"

"But this Jesus is as dangerous to Herod as he is to us!" exclaimed the scribe.

"That may be true, but just the same Herod knows that the people like Jesus," said Symeon. "Still, I am sure the king would put a quick end to this small-town prophet if it could be done without stirring up the people."

"Look, my friend," declared the scribe. "You know as well as I do that these common folk will not follow anyone who goes too far for them. From what you have told me, we ought not to have much trouble showing these simple Galileans that he is not a loyal Jew at all."

Symeon laughed bitterly. "Every day he breaks the tradition a hundred times!" A frown came over his face. "The trouble is —the people like it!"

"That may be partly true," admitted the scribe. "But I believe these country people are still real Jews at heart. They may be crude and uneducated, but they will never follow anyone who is trying to destroy the Law and break down our religion. The Nazarene can break a regulation here and there, and they like it—yes! But let him say anything against Moses, or Abraham, or the great Rabbis—they will desert him by the hundreds!"

"If that happened, Herod would throw the whole band of them in prison without delay," replied Symeon enthusiastically. "I believe you have struck on the way to stop this false Rabbi!"

The scribe lowered his voice. "When do you think we could find him with some of his followers?"

"He is always at the lake in the morning," replied Symeon.

About ten o'clock the next day, the men stepped into the sunlit street in front of Symeon's home. Over their shoulders each wore a short cape, beautifully decorated with four blue tassels, one at each corner. Many Jews wore this cape, but only the Pharisees added extra long blue tassels.

They descended the cobblestone street from the high part of Capernaum where Symeon lived and went toward the lake below. People bowed and smiled, but the two men paid no attention. They were used to having people make way for them. They strode into the crowded market place, already hot under the rays of the morning sun. The hoofs of many animals had raised a cloud of dust. Everywhere farmers and fishermen were shouting, trying to catch the ear of persons who came to buy. Only the donkeys, laboring under huge baskets of food, refused to budge for the officials.

After a short walk through the narrow streets of Capernaum, Symeon caught sight of the lake, blue and cool, dancing in the sunlight. He pointed ahead of them. "The Nazarene is usually on the shore a little way beyond those fishing boats." They were approaching a group of fishermen who had drawn up their boats and spread nets on the beach.

"We must show these people that he is not merely meddling with parts of the Law," remarked the scribe. "The fact is that he is not a true Jew at all!"

A group of people had gathered on the shore, just to the right of the road. "There they are!" exclaimed Symeon.

The two men stopped briefly at the edge of the circle of people and then walked boldly up to Jesus. Seeing their robes, everyone made way. "It is widely reported, Rabbi," said the scribe, "that your disciples do not keep all the sacred customs of our religion."

Jesus answered them the same way he spoke to the common people that sat around him. "Where do your customs come from?" he asked directly.

Just the opening they wanted! The scribe did not miss his chance.

"Moses himself gave us these commands," he declared. "Yet I heard that your disciples do not wash their hands before meals as Moses commanded us."

Without a moment's hesitation Jesus retorted: "Have you forgotten that Moses also commanded you to honor your father and your mother? Yet you have made up a rule that allows a rich man to say to his aged parents, 'I can't support you—I have given all my money to God.' The fact is that he has not given it to God at all; he has only paid a fee to the priests!" Jesus was indignant. "You talk about Moses, but you yourselves break his commands!"

The scribe had to defend himself. "This rule was made by one of our great rabbis," he said.

"You have put human rules in the place of the commands of God," declared Jesus. "Isaiah was talking about you when he said, 'These people give me respect with their mouths, but their hearts are far away from me!' "

"Do you dare attack the great Rabbis?" demanded the scribe angrily. "Every true Jew at least respects their words. Yet you say that a man need not purify his hands before he eats!"

"It is not what goes into a man's mouth that hurts him," replied Jesus, quietly. "It is the things that come out of a man—his words and deeds—that harm him."

"Are you saying that we should disobey this law?" retorted the scribe. "Moses himself gave us this command!"

"You cannot find eternal life just by keeping rules," replied Jesus. The watching people wondered at his calmness. "If you are really in search of the Kingdom of God, repent!"

Dramatically the scribe turned to the people. "Do you see?" he demanded. "This man is not one of us! He wants to change the laws that Moses has given us! He is dangerous—do not believe him!" He stalked through the awe-struck crowd and left, followed by Symeon.

For a long time, Jesus sat silently before the people. By the time he finally spoke, they were all wondering what he could say.

"The door of the Kingdom of Heaven is open to anyone who will put his trust in God," said Jesus quietly. "The scribes and Pharisees claim that they keep the Law of Moses. They say they speak with God's authority. Do what they tell you if you want to—but do not act the way they do! They have made so many rules for you that no one can obey them all! Do they help you enter the Kingdom? No! They make life easy for themselves and impossible for all others! They do all they can to attract attention. Every day their tassels get longer! They sit in the most important places at feasts! They love the front seats at the synagogue! How they enjoy having people step out of their way and say, 'Good morning, teacher'! Men who belong to God's Kingdom do not want to be called Rabbi; they are all brothers and have only one Father, God in heaven." He stood up. "Let us leave this place," he said.

Simon fell in step with Jesus as they turned toward Capernaum. The sun was still as bright; the waves on the lake danced as merrily as before, but the disciples took no joy in the beauty of the day.

"Master, those men are trying to set the people against us," said Simon, deeply concerned.

"They can do nothing against God," replied Jesus.

"But they are deceiving many people," warned Simon.

"Anyone who will believe them is blind to my gospel," said Jesus sadly. "Let them follow these blind leaders, if they insist —they will come to the same bad end!"

It soon became plain that Simon was right: the scribe's attack on Jesus was having a serious effect. The next day each of the twelve disciples went to a different place in Capernaum to preach the news of the Kingdom of God. At the end of the afternoon, Andrew stopped to visit a fisherman whom he had known since childhood. "The men ought to be coming in from the lake soon," observed the wife of Andrew's friend. The dogs outside began to bark. "There they are now!"

"Andrew!" An older man entered. "I am glad to see you. What is this I hear about you these days?" He sat down for a moment before washing. "Have you been getting along all right since you left your fishing? What is your Master doing? I hear some very bad rumors!"

Andrew was taken back. "Why, I don't know what you mean."

"Well, perhaps I should not have mentioned it," the old fisherman said. "But I thought you could tell me the truth, if anyone could."

"What have you heard?" asked Andrew, puzzled.

"Everyone is talking about your Rabbi," answered the man. "Is it true, what they are saying?"

"I know nothing about it," said Andrew.

"I thought you would have heard," said the man, hesitating. "One of the fishermen who listens to Jesus told us today that he intends to destroy the Jewish religion!"

"That is nonsense!" cried Andrew. "Where did he ever . . ." Suddenly it came to him: This was what the scribe was telling people! "Look here," said Andrew with great earnestness. "Do you really think that Jesus is trying to keep people from believing in God and serving him?"

"Oh, I didn't say that!" laughed the old fisherman. "I was only telling you what I heard." A questioning tone came into his voice. "But he *does* say that you do not have to obey Moses, doesn't he?"

Andrew did not know what to answer. It was true that Jesus had said there were more important things than purifying the hands before eating!

"There is something else I heard," continued the older man. "How could a really great Rabbi come from Nazareth? That town does not amount to anything."

"What difference does it make where he comes from?" protested Andrew.

The old man shrugged and stood up. "It is a serious matter for your Jesus to say all the great Rabbis are wrong. I always wondered if you knew what you were doing when you gave up fishing." He looked keenly at Andrew. "Today I took time off to go to listen to him myself. He talks as if he knew more about God's will than Moses did! He goes too far for me. After all, I am a Jew!" Abruptly he changed the subject. "Will you stay for supper, Andrew?"

"No . . . no. I think I had better be going," murmured Andrew. Hurriedly he left. He was much upset by the words of this trusted friend. Purple shadows filled the narrow streets. Most of the people were already indoors. Andrew felt terribly alone. In his haste he tripped over a broken cart wheel and he was startled by its loud clatter on the paving. He began to run. He was relieved to get to Simon's home.

Jesus had not yet returned, but Andrew found the other disciples in the midst of a serious conversation. "Everything the Master does proves that God's power is in him," John was saying. "We need him! Everybody in this city needs him!"

Andrew burst out: "Have you heard what people are saying? That scribe is telling everyone that we are trying to wipe out the whole Jewish religion!"

"That is what we are talking about," said Simon. Andrew sat down as Simon turned to John. "Of course, it is true that the Master really does put his own teaching above the command of Moses."

"I know he does," answered John passionately, "and he is right! What should we do without him? We have already given up everything to follow him!" He jumped to his feet and began to pace back and forth.

"Many people are leaving us," said James, greatly worried. "We shall soon have nobody."

"Can he really be right and all the Rabbis and Pharisees and scribes wrong?" exclaimed Andrew. "If he were the Messiah, I should feel different, but . . ." He stopped. The other men were staring at him. The Messiah!

At that moment Jesus entered the room. He saw James's anxiety. John stopped walking. Andrew was flushed with excitement. His last remark had stamped an expression of amazement and doubt on the faces of all the men.

"My followers," said Jesus, grasping their thoughts immediately, "do not be troubled. You believe in God, believe also in me." He sat in the midst of them. "God has sent me into the world with the light of his gospel. I have not come to condemn the world, but to save people from darkness. If they do not believe my word, that is because they love darkness better than the light." John went back to his place and slumped down. "Those who are truly seeking God know that our gospel is true and come to us," continued Jesus. "But those who turn away from us do it for just one reason: their lives are evil. It is true that they obey many laws and seem very religious, but their hearts are proud. They do not really depend on God. They do not live close to him. They cannot endure the truth which shows them that they are in darkness."

After a long silence, Andrew rose and walked out into the cool night. He looked up at the clear stars and wondered how

long it would be before they would look down on a happy nation, ruled by God's Messiah. The turmoil in his heart had
quieted while Jesus spoke. The new moon, thin as a curved
sword, gleamed high above. A faint wind rattled the palms on
the street in front of the house. Simon came out.

"What if everyone leaves us, Simon?" asked Andrew abruptly.

Simon's answer was firm. "He is the only one who has a message of eternal life. If we leave him, to whom can we go?"

Jesus had seen how terribly disturbed the disciples were by
the criticisms against him. Therefore, very early the next morning before the people began to come to market, he took them
to the lake. They had no idea where he was leading them as
they stepped into Simon's boat.

What a relief it was to be away from the crowds of Capernaum! They were glad for the silence of the lake, smooth as a
mirror in the calm of the dawn, after the noise and bustle of
street and market. Through the mist the men could see a few
fishermen working hard to gather in their nets with the night's
catch of fish. Simon and Andrew recognized them, but the men
did not look up and the disciples passed unseen. In the days
when they too had gathered nets in the morning the four fishermen had always been glad to feel the warming rays of the sun
breaking through the blanket of fog. The mist began now to
tear into ragged pieces, clinging here and there to the lake. The
disciples caught sight of the stately crest of Mount Hermon to
the north, white with summer snow, standing guard over all
Galilee. A breeze sprang up and blew the remaining mist to
tatters. Little wisps of fog chased each other over the surface
of the water as though ashamed to be caught by the sun.

Jesus turned his gaze from the noble mountain ahead of
them and spoke to the disciples. "I must warn you against the
tricks of the Pharisees and scribes. Their false arguments sometimes sound reasonable, but the evil purpose of these men grows
like a nasty mold. It will creep into your very hearts and destroy
the Bread of Life."

James leaned over to Philip. "That reminds me—did you
bring enough food for this trip?"

"The provisions ought to be stored under the stern seat," answered Philip.

James reached under the seat. "Nothing here," he said.

"What! No food?" The other disciples had heard what he said. They were hungry. They forgot that Jesus was speaking. "Look under the front seat, Andrew," said Simon. The men searched everywhere; there was but one loaf in the boat. James turned to Philip in a temper. "What in the world are we going to eat?"

Jesus had watched them without saying a word. Now he spoke. "My followers, what have you to worry about?"

"This stupid Philip forgot to bring the food!" said James, irritated.

"Have you ever gone hungry when you were with me?" asked Jesus patiently. "You have seen me feed crowds—and yet you do not trust me! Many times you have heard me say that I am the Bread of Life—and now you are worried about your stomachs!" Tempers cooled as quickly as they had risen. "Do you not understand the meaning of the things I do?" asked Jesus.

"You are right, Master," said James, shamefaced. "We should not worry about food."

"Is that all I mean to you?" asked Jesus. "You do not understand why I fed the people, do you?"

Simon and John brought the boat to land at a deserted spot near the fishing village of Bethsaida, and Jesus led the men north along the Jordan toward the Lebanon Mountains. For three days they traveled, finally reaching the narrow valleys of the foothills of the Lebanons. The land was hilly but very fertile. Many people lived here: a few Jews but many gentiles. The disciples had never traveled this far north before. As the mountains grew higher, they turned westward toward the Mediterranean Sea. Jesus chose this road because he believed he could find privacy in which to teach the disciples.

However, things were not as Jesus hoped. About ten miles from Sidon, a gentile city on the seacoast, they passed through a small village. The disciples thought they had not been recognized, but a short distance beyond the town John said, "There is someone following us!"

The others glanced around. A woman was coming after them. "Let us hurry on," said Simon. "Perhaps she will drop back." All of them quickened their pace. After a moment Simon glanced around again. "She is running after us!"

The woman cried out: "O thou Son of David! Have pity on me!"

Jesus paid no attention. "Have mercy on me, Son of David!" cried the woman desperately. "My daughter has an evil spirit!"

Still Jesus walked on. "Send her away, Master," said Simon. "She is just going to keep on wailing behind us."

Jesus stopped. "God has sent me only to the lost sheep of the flock of Israel."

"And she is a gentile," said James with satisfaction. When the woman overtook them, he was sure Jesus would send her away.

Kneeling, the woman said, "Do help me, Lord!"

The disciples were taken back. How did she dare call him "Lord"! Who did she think he was?

When Jesus spoke to the woman his voice was kindly, but the words seemed harsh: "Woman, it is not fair to take the children's food and throw it to the dogs under the table."

That will show her she has no right to bother us, thought James.

But James was mistaken. "No, Master," the woman answered smiling, "but the dogs can wait patiently for the crumbs to fall from the children's table, can't they?"

Jesus' face lighted up. "O woman, you have great faith! You have found the Kingdom of God. Go back to your daughter; your prayer is granted."

The disciples were aghast. James burst out, "Master, what can this mean?"

"How can a gentile be included in our Kingdom?" demanded Simon.

"Do you not yet understand why I have come?" answered Jesus. "My Father sent me to declare that all who are far away from him may come back if they will repent. The Kingdom of God belongs to anyone who will come."

"But that cannot mean all the gentiles," protested Simon.

"You have forgotten what the Prophet Hosea once said," replied Jesus. "To certain people it was said at one time, 'You do not belong to God'—but now these very people are the children of God!' There was finality in Jesus' voice, and the disciples could say nothing more as the woman went home to her daughter.

Jesus knew from their sullen silence that the disciples resented his kindness to the gentile woman. He saw Simon, Andrew, and James drop behind the group.

"How can he do a thing like that?" fumed Simon. "He came to help outcasts—but not gentiles!"

"She had the impudence to call him 'Lord'!" remarked Andrew.

Nevertheless, not one of them dared complain against Jesus even though they went on talking among themselves after they left the country around Sidon. Jesus made it so hard for them to follow him! Yet they were bound to him, and nothing could drive them away.

Jesus did not enter Sidon, but turned back toward the mountain passes that led toward Caesarea Philippi, a city near the foot of Mount Hermon. The disciples had preached the good news of the Kingdom in the villages of upper Galilee, and every day they saw people that they recognized. But something seemed to be wrong. When they had preached before, the people had welcomed them with joy. But now people hardly even greeted them! What had happened? Had they forgotten the Rabbi from Nazareth who had healed their sick? Where were the people who had said that Jesus had changed their lives and given them new hope?

"Have the rumors about us spread here too?" asked James in despair.

"Do you wonder the people think he goes to extremes?" asked James bitterly. "If they knew he told a gentile woman she could share in our Kingdom, everyone would turn away from us!"

"Sometimes it almost seems as though the scribes were right!" confessed Andrew.

Simon caught him up instantly. "Do you think that Jesus is trying to destroy the faith of our nation?" he asked sharply. Andrew did not answer.

"Why did we follow him in the first place, brother?" urged Simon. Still Andrew said nothing—but he knew what Simon meant.

"Should we go back to our fishing, Andrew?"

"Oh, no!" answered Andrew, thinking of the hopeless years before Jesus came. "That could never be."

"God has sent him to open a new day for us!" declared Simon firmly.

Jesus had been walking with Philip, but now he dropped back beside the other disciples. The road lay between high rock walls. Their footsteps rang with a hollow sound. The shadows were deep; no other travelers were in sight. James said quietly, "We were just talking about what people are saying, Master."

"What do they say about me?" asked Jesus. Simon knew that he sensed the discouragement and doubt of his followers.

"The Pharisees say that you are trying to break down the Law of Moses," replied John hesitantly. There was a long silence.

"Some people think you are John the Baptizer risen from the dead," added Andrew.

The Zealot said: "I hear some saying that you are Elijah come down from heaven to prepare the way of the Messiah. That is what I thought at first." A tiny stream of water, flowing over a rock, could be heard in the silence that followed the Zealot's remark.

"What else do people say about me?" persisted Jesus.

"Many people think that you are a prophet, Master," answered Simon.

Jesus looked quietly at the men around him. When he spoke his words came deliberately. His voice was strong and deep. "But, Simon, who do you believe I am?"

To Simon, Jesus' question was like a powerful beam of light shining into the darkest corners of his mind, driving away the last black shadows of doubt. With a sigh he raised his head and caught sight of the brilliant blue sky high above the dark valley that shut them in. The answer to his Master's question was as clear as that sunny sky—why had he not known it before? Simon's lips moved; then came his answer: "You are the Christ, the Son of the living God."

11. A SECRET IS TOLD

Y̲ou are the Christ—the Son of the living God!" Against the high rock walls of the narrow ravine, the words echoed in the disciples' ears. For many months not one of them had dared to say that he believed this was true—but now Simon had confessed it plainly.

"Simon," declared Jesus, "unless God had taught you this, you could never have known it. From this time on your name will be Peter, the Rock. On the solid rock of faith like yours, I will build my Church—and nothing shall ever destroy it!

"Whoever puts his faith in God is a member of my Kingdom. To you"—he looked around at all the disciples now—"I have entrusted the keys to the door of my Kingdom. If you teach men to believe in me, they shall enter!"

"We will tell every Jew that you are the Messiah!" burst out the Zealot enthusiastically.

"No!" declared Jesus firmly. "This must remain a complete secret."

The disciples were dumfounded. "But, Master," protested Andrew, "a Messiah whom nobody knows can never lead the people!"

"Now is the time for action!" exclaimed the Zealot.

"I have work to do which you do not understand," answered Jesus. "I have come to save the people—but in order to do it, I must first endure much suffering."

"We are ready to fight for you," answered Judas.

"It will cost more than that," replied Jesus. "I will be rejected by the high priest, the Pharisees, the scribes—and every authority in our nation."

"We can overcome them if we have to," said the Zealot impatiently.

The answer came like an exploding bomb. "They are going to kill me," declared Jesus plainly.

The men looked at him speechless. "They may try to kill you," blurted Andrew, "but they can never do it!"

"I must die," repeated Jesus. "There is no other way for me to finish the work that God sent me to do."

A great force rose within Simon Peter; words flooded his lips. "No! This cannot be! God would never let it happen! He has sent you to lead us! You cannot die!"

Jesus' stern voice cut him short, "Get behind me, Satan! You are not on the side of God when you talk like that. You make it harder for me to do what I was sent to do! If I were to do what you want, I could never do my Father's work!"

"Master, how can you say such a thing!" protested Andrew, defending his brother.

"You do not know God's purpose," answered Jesus, turning quickly. "You have your own idea about what I should do— but you do not know the will of God!" Then Jesus spoke with great force to all the disciples. "I am not going to lead you to the victory you expect. If you are determined to follow me, you will suffer. No one who seeks worldly gain is fit to be my disciple. But if you are willing to lose your life for my sake—then you will find eternal life!"

Peter was humiliated. To think that the Master could accuse him of serving the evil one!

"Peter," said Jesus, now gentle, "the people of Israel have many needs—but I am sent to bring them eternal life in his Kingdom." Peter sat with his eyes cast down. Jesus spoke to all the men.

"There was once a time when I was tempted to preach some other message," continued Jesus. "Soon after I was baptized by John in the Jordan River, I went alone into the wilderness to pray and to seek the will of the Heavenly Father. For forty days I fasted. The Tempter came to me in a vision and said to me, 'If you are really the Son of God, turn this stone into bread!' I could have great power over men if I were willing to satisfy the desires of these hungry people!" The disciples remembered how Jesus had refused to listen to the five thousand people who tried to make him their king.

"But I could not do that," continued Jesus. "I remembered what the Scriptures say: 'Man does not live only on bread—but on every word of truth which comes from God.'" Peter was looking at Jesus attentively.

"Then in my vision Satan took me to the highest spire on the roof of the Temple in Jerusalem," continued Jesus. "'Leap down!' he said, 'you will not be hurt: Aren't you the Messiah? The angels will protect you! When these people see you do such a marvelous miracle they will all fall down and worship you!'" Jesus paused. "Do you see why this was wrong? The Father does not give me special protection. He did not send me into the world to astonish people with miracles so that they will accept me—he has sent me to tell them his message of life!" The disciples again remembered another thing Jesus had refused to do: he would not perform a miracle for the Pharisees! "No man submits to the rule of God just because you amaze him with miracles!"

Jesus spoke now to Peter. "Finally Satan took me to the top of a great mountain where we could see every nation in the world. In my vision I saw all the people who were oppressed by unjust kings. I saw all the wealth and power of the earth. Then Satan whispered in my ear, 'I will give you power to do anything you wish—to help people all you want—if you will give up this plan to proclaim the rule of God and will worship me!' " Worship Satan! The idea sent a chill through the disciples.

"I did not come to set up a new empire on earth," declared Jesus, turning to the Zealot. "That is not what God sent me to do! We must not do our own will, but the will of the Father in heaven! I am here to proclaim an eternal Kingdom!" There was a long silence. "So I answered Satan, 'You shall worship the Lord your God, and him only shall you serve.' "

Peter now understood why Jesus had rebuked him. "But if you die?" he asked. "How can you give men eternal life if you die?"

"The Kingdom of God will come in great power when the Son of Man has risen from the dead," declared Jesus.

The disciples were not sure what the Master meant by his last remark. They had more than enough to think about. After a few minutes they climbed out of the deep valley. Before them lay rolling woodland cut into sections by deep ravines which carried swift streams to the Jordan. It was very different from the rocky hills the disciples had traveled since leaving the territory around Sidon.

"The Jordan River lies over there," said Simon, pointing east. The men paused and looked while they caught their breath. Heavy trees hanging over the edge of the deep river gorge concealed the stream itself.

"Do we have to go through there?" inquired John. He remembered stories that travelers told about this wild country: lions and wolves lurked in the heavy growth of trees that covered the cliffs and gullies.

"If we go to Caesarea Philippi, we will," answered the Zealot. He was familiar with this part of the country, having traveled through it before as far east as Damascus. John looked inquiringly at Jesus.

"We will travel back to Capernaum in a few days," said Jesus. "But first we will go over toward Caesarea Philippi." He led them down the slope.

"I do not blame him for not wanting to go back to Galilee right away," remarked Andrew as they walked.

"The people certainly do not follow him as they once did," agreed Simon.

"Things are not as bad as he thinks," said Andrew. "There are many people who would go anywhere with us. These scribes have turned some people against us, but we can win them back!"

Simon shook his head. "Perhaps. But the Master has usually known what to expect. He has not been wrong other times."

"Oh, I am sure it is just discouragement!" insisted Andrew. "He will get over it."

Peter, however, was not satisfied. All the way down through the deep ravines that descended to the Jordan he said nothing. The sun was behind the hills by the time the disciples entered the dense growth of trees. The road was narrow, and they had to pick their way with care because of roots and overhanging branches. John looked fearfully from left to right as they went farther and farther into the forest.

"I don't think it is very safe in here at night," he whispered to James. Several of the men were keeping a sharp watch, peering into the trees and turning to look behind. They wondered if Jesus knew that the tangled undergrowth might conceal vicious animals.

"He must want to cross the river before nightfall," answered James.

Peter and Andrew took no notice of the blackness of the jungle. At last Peter said: "The Master does not get easily discouraged. He means more than we think when he says he is going to die. He will tell us plainly if we ask him."

"Oh, let's not talk to him now!" replied Andrew quickly. "I think we understand."

Peter looked at him narrowly. "We ought to ask him, Andrew," he insisted. "We must be sure!"

"There is time enough later on." Andrew was evasive.

"I believe you are afraid of what he might say!" Andrew would not meet his brother's eyes. "Come with me!" Almost by force, Peter pulled his brother along until they had overtaken Jesus.

"Master," said Peter, "tell us plainly what you meant by saying that you must die."

"If I go straight on with the task God has given me to do, I shall be killed. You know what the Prophet says about God's servant: 'He was despised, and rejected of men.'"

"But, Master," interrupted Andrew, "what good can dying do? If you are killed, how can we ever save the Jews?"

"Not even the Son knows the will of the Father in some matters," replied Jesus. "God's servants cannot always understand him. He asks us only to obey and trust him."

"You take away every hope!" cried Andrew. "What is going to become of us?"

Peter put his arm across his brother's shoulder to restrain him.

"Anyone who wants to save his own life will surely lose it," said Jesus gently. "But if you are willing to lose your life for my sake, you will find true life."

Andrew's mind was whirling. He could not grasp the meaning of Jesus' words. Only Peter's strong grip on his shoulder kept him from answering with senseless protests.

They dropped behind the others and Andrew burst out: "We are wrong! All this time we have been wrong!" He looked desperately at Peter and whispered, "Let us go back to our fishing boats, brother!" They stood facing each other in a little clearing.

Andrew's panic shook Peter deeply. "Then you do believe that the scribes and Pharisees are right, Andrew?" But his brother would not answer.

"Do you think that the Master's power comes from Satan?" Peter asked again.

Andrew sat down heavily on a rock at the side of the road and buried his face in his hands. Peter could hear him breathing hard as he murmured, "Oh, I cannot escape from him—but I cannot understand him!"

The other disciples had disappeared into the woods on the opposite edge of the open glade. Their footsteps quickly died away. The silence of the murky forest settled around the two fishermen. Tears came through Andrew's fingers, but he made no sound. He did not observe that they were alone.

"Come, brother," Peter urged anxiously, "we must hurry. The others are getting ahead of us. This forest is dangerous after dark."

Peter was greatly relieved when he and Andrew finally caught up with the others. A half hour later the men emerged from the forest and climbed the slope that enclosed the basin of the Jordan on the eastern side of the river. Their sandals were wet from fording the river, but they hardly noticed it, so relieved were they to be once again in open country.

It was almost totally dark now. Only dimly could they make out the bulk of Mount Hermon rising directly ahead of them, hiding the evening star. Jesus led the tired men to an inn.

"He must have intended to lead us here," exclaimed John, catching sight of the faint glimmer of a lamp in the courtyard of the building. He, Peter, and James stayed in a single tiny room.

"This has been a hard day," remarked James wearily, stretching out on the bed.

"I do not believe we shall leave Galilee again until we go to Jerusalem," observed Peter.

"I wish we knew what would happen there," remarked John. "Do you think he will really be killed?"

"You know what Andrew says," replied Peter, avoiding a direct answer.

"I cannot believe that the Master is just discouraged," stated James flatly. "That is not like him."

Peter nodded his agreement. He thought of how Andrew was inwardly torn. "I cannot escape from him—but I cannot understand him!" he had said. James blew out the oil lamp. The men settled themselves for the night. Peter spoke. "If we follow him to Jerusalem, we must be ready to suffer with him. We must not doubt."

"Tell me, Simon Peter, how can the Messiah of God die?" asked James.

The fishermen heard Peter sigh. "How it can be . . . I do not know. I know only that we must decide whether we shall go on. Now is the time to decide . . ." His voice trailed off. Far into the night the fishermen stared open-eyed into the darkness. When at last they fell into a troubled sleep, they were no nearer the answer.

At dawn there was a knock at the door of their room. The men stirred, and Peter rose. Scarcely visible in the faint light stood Jesus. Peter stepped back, and Jesus entered.

"Will you come to pray with me in the mountain?" Jesus asked.

The men dressed and followed Jesus outside. The road on which the inn was built lay at the foot of Mount Hermon. Its snowy crest rose majestically above them, shining brilliantly in the morning sun. A few days before, the fishermen had seen this peak above the mist that lay over the Lake of Galilee.

The beauty of the mountain would have lifted the spirits of men whose hearts were less heavy, but Peter, James, and John had awakened with the same anxiety that had troubled their rest. They did not talk, but climbed steadily toward the summit of the mountain.

At last Jesus stopped. Below them lay the valleys of Galilee. Far to the south a blanket of fog covered the lake. As Peter looked, he could not keep back his homesickness; on the shore of that misty lake lived his wife and children. The flood of sunlight had gradually crept down the slope toward them, and now the four men felt its warmth. "Let us kneel here and pray," said Jesus.

While Jesus and the three fishermen were away in the mountain, a strange scene occurred at the inn where the other nine disciples had just awakened. Early travelers were moving along the road in front of the inn. Among them came a man leading a donkey on which a boy was riding. He stopped at the inn.

"Has Jesus of Nazareth passed this way?" he asked the innkeeper, who was standing there.

"Haven't heard anything about him," answered the man curtly. Suddenly he shouted, "Watch out!" The boy was falling off the donkey. His father leaped to catch him, but the donkey shied away and the boy fell heavily to the ground and lay still.

"Ah, my son!" cried the father. He lifted the child gently and carried him toward the inn.

"Here, you!" shouted the owner roughly. "Get that boy out of here. He has a devil!"

The father hesitated and then started toward a long bench. "Let me lay him here," he begged.

"Well, all right," grumbled the innkeeper. "But don't take him inside."

People had heard the noise and were looking out of the windows. Philip and the Zealot came through the doorway.

"What is the matter with your son?" they asked sympathetically.

"He has falling sickness," answered the man. "He often hurts himself this way." He was wiping blood from a cut on the boy's pale forehead. The lad opened his eyes and tried to rise.

"Stay there, my son," urged the father. He turned to Philip and the Zealot. "Can you tell me where I can find Jesus of Nazareth? I have heard wonderful reports of his power to heal."

The two disciples glanced at each other. At that moment Judas and Levi came out of the inn.

"This man is looking for the Master," said Philip.

"Are you his followers?" cried the man. "I have traveled for five days to find you! If only you will heal my son!"

Travelers had stopped and clustered around the lad on the bench. Almost all the guests at the inn had come outside. The four disciples looked at one another; none offered to heal the boy.

"Some of you visited my own village and healed many who had evil spirits," said the father hopefully. He could not understand why the men hesitated. They still made no move toward the boy. Andrew came out of the inn.

"Can you heal my son?" the man asked Andrew. Andrew glanced at the others. He knew why they hung back. He looked at the boy. The father's voice was urgent. The people watched intently as Andrew stepped up to the boy, lying limp but conscious.

"Be gone from him!" commanded Andrew, as though speaking to an evil spirit in the boy. A shiver ran through his body, but then he lay still again.

Scornful smiles curled the lips of the people who watched. A great healer, this man! He tells the devil to leave and the boy is worse off than before!

Andrew flamed scarlet—but he was not thinking of the bystanders. In his heart he knew he was powerless to help the boy. The father bent over his son and then suddenly stood up. "You cannot help him! You have no power!"

Andrew was stunned. For a moment he stood stock-still. Then he turned and walked away.

"A fine proof of the power of the Nazarene!" remarked a man sarcastically. The people recognized him as a priest who had stopped a few minutes before to watch. The father of the boy looked around at the people, desperately seeking someone else to help him.

"Where is your Master?" cried the father desperately.

"Yes, where is your Master?" echoed the priest in derision. "You had better go and find him!"

"He left a couple hours ago with three others," said the innkeeper, in a very matter-of-fact way. "He went up there." He waved toward the great mountain. The people looked where he pointed.

"There he is!" cried a man in the crowd. Distant figures were moving down the mountainside.

"Now we shall see if this Nazarene can do better than his followers," remarked the priest bitingly.

As Jesus approached, he took in the whole scene at a glance: the sick boy, the despairing father, the sneering official, and the beaten disciples.

"O sir, my son has a terrible sickness!" said the father. "He even falls into the fire and hurts himself." He gave a pitiable little gesture toward his son, stretched on the bench. "Your disciples could not help him at all!"

Jesus turned to his disciples. They looked at him dully. Andrew stood a distance away; his face clearly showed his humiliation.

Jesus' voice had in it more of weariness and sorrow than sharpness. "How utterly faithless you are! You turn your backs on God himself! How long must I teach you? How much longer must I endure your cold hearts?" He turned to the man.

"How long has your son been like this?"

"From the time he was a little child," replied the father. "If you can do anything at all, help us! Do have pity on us!"

"Why do you say, 'If you can'? Do you not believe that I can heal this boy? Anything can be done for one who has real faith!" The disciples knew that Jesus might as well have been speaking to them.

"O Master," the man cried passionately, "I really do believe! Help me to be rid of my doubt and fear!"

Andrew realized that the man was like himself: torn between faith and doubt. "Master, help me to believe too," murmured Andrew.

Jesus turned to the boy and spoke to him. He gave a loud cry and then relaxed.

"He is dead!" the father exclaimed.

Jesus stooped and took the pale hand of the youth. Immediately he sat up; then to the astonishment of everyone he stood.

Jesus did not wait for the father's thanks. He did not even glance at the crowd, but turned to his disciples.

"You had no power because you had no faith," he said directly. "If you truly believe in God, evil cannot stand against you. Without faith, you are helpless. But even the tiniest bit of real trust is mighty enough to change the whole world!"

12. THE GREATEST AMONG US

THE next morning the disciples could not help noticing that
Peter acted differently. He had been as downcast and silent
yesterday as the rest—but now he was talking eagerly with James
and John as they walked ahead of the other men.

"If John the Baptizer really was Elijah," exclaimed Peter,
"then the Kingdom ought to be very near!"

"Will John be raised from the dead?" asked James.

"Jesus said that the Messiah would rise," remarked Peter.

James said, "I don't see what he could mean by that."

"Do you remember the voice from the cloud?" interrupted
John. "Those were the same words that he heard when he was
baptized: 'You are my beloved Son!' Only this time we heard the
voice too."

"It said, 'Listen to him!' " Peter's voice showed the awe he felt. "I don't know what this vision means, but I am sure he is the Messiah himself!"

James and John did not reply. They needed their breath because they were climbing a steep hill.

When they reached the crest, all the Twelve stopped to rest. The road had gradually turned east, and now the green lowlands of the upper Jordan Valley lay behind them. But the men did not look back; they had eyes only for the gleaming city that lay in the shallow valley ahead of them, Caesarea Philippi. Beyond the domes and colonnades of the city rose more mountains, ridge after ridge, climbing finally to the snowy crest of the range, over nine thousand feet above. The level valley before them, however, was green and fertile. Groves of trees and neatly planted fields reached to the very edge of the foothills on all sides of the city. Caesarea Philippi seemed like a diamond set among green jewels.

The columns of several pagan temples reminded the travelers that this lovely city was the home of Philip, the son of Herod the Great. He had spent much money to make it beautiful. But the disciples found little pleasure in the sight.

"Heathen people building temples to worship idols!" murmured James. As the men descended the hill they walked along the foot of a high cliff, rising to their left.

"We will not enter this city," said Jesus. The men knew that a road branched to the south toward Lake Huleh, which was not far from the Lake of Galilee. John happened to look up at the cliff. "Where does the water come from that runs down here?" he asked curiously. Shrubs of all kinds clung to crannies in the damp rock wall.

"Perhaps there is an underground stream," replied James, hopefully. They were all thirsty. A moment later he saw a deep pool almost hidden at the very foot of the cliff. "There it is!" he exclaimed. Several of the men started toward the spring.

"Wait!" called Peter sharply. He pointed up at the face of the cliff. James looked up and saw that a deep hole had been carved in the rock. It was framed by two stone columns and a stone arch. Under the arch stood a statue of Pan, the pagan god of nature.

"Stop!" cried Peter. "That water is unholy!" The other disciples caught sight of the idol and shrank back.

"This place is defiled!" exclaimed James in disgust. "We cannot drink this water!" The presence of the idol was an offense to the men and they deeply resented it.

"Just wait until we get control of this land again!" burst out the Zealot. "We will break these filthy images to pieces!"

"Just to think that the land of God's promise is filled with heathen idols!" Peter was seething. He turned to Jesus. "How much longer must we endure this?"

James interrupted. "It will not be long, will it, Master?"

"Can we start for Jerusalem soon?" urged the Zealot. "Surely the time has come for God to deliver his people!" Jesus said nothing, but led them over the crest of a ridge till Caesarea Philippi disappeared behind them. The road descended into a flat swamp land which reached as far south as Lake Huleh, which they could now see. The air was heavy with moist heat, and the people they passed looked unhealthy.

The disciples scarcely noticed their discomfort, however, so eager was their conversation. Again they tried to make Jesus promise that he would use his power soon to conquer the Romans, but Jesus refused to join in their discussion of how they would rule the land when the Romans were beaten. Not one of them remembered his solemn warnings about the suffering which they faced. Not one mentioned that Jesus had said he would be killed in Jerusalem.

Judas listened and said little. Finally he could stand their conversation no longer. "How many of you have ever lived in Jerusalem?" he asked, breaking in.

"I stayed there a few weeks once," said James, puzzled by his question.

"I used to go every year when I was a boy," said Levi.

"Do you know any people who live in Jerusalem?" asked Judas.

"John and I know some people we sold fish to," answered Andrew.

Judas could hardly keep the scorn out of his voice. "You don't know the first thing about Jerusalem! You have no idea what you are getting into! You don't know anyone there except a few low-class people!"

The Zealot interrupted. "You seem to forget that I have a large number of friends in Jerusalem," he said hotly. "The city is full of Zealots! They all know me."

"Yes, and the police keep track of every one of them," retorted Judas. "Just as soon as the Romans see us with Zealots they will think that we are trying to start trouble. The best thing for us to do is to keep away from your friends!"

"I suppose you think we will win the confidence of the Jews by mixing with Pharisees!" snapped the Zealot.

"We will have to be careful, of course," said Judas. "But I know the right people. If we are clever, we will work from the inside."

"Well, I think the Master knows what he is doing," cut in Andrew.

Judas glanced ahead to where Jesus was walking alone and lowered his voice. "You know I am loyal to him, but he has been in Jerusalem only a few times in his life. He doesn't know any of the important people."

"I can put him in touch with hundreds of men who will fight beside us," said the Zealot, frowning at Judas. As Andrew listened to the two men argue, he had to admit to himself that Jesus might need help when they came to Jerusalem. He did not say any more.

The twelve men and their Master came to a ford where a sluggish stream flowed across the road toward the Jordan. Single file, the disciples waded through the shallowest place. Andrew was the last to cross, and he found himself with Peter, James, and John. The four fishermen let the others walk ahead. Keeping his voice low, James said to the others: "What is going to happen to the rest of us when we get to Jerusalem? Those two men have been there and they know everyone! We might even be pushed out completely!" The more they discussed it, the more worried they became.

James and John wanted to be alone to talk about the schemes

of Judas and the Zealot, so when the Twelve stopped for lunch, they went to a near-by farm to buy food. After lunch they again fell in step with Andrew and Peter.

"You were absolutely right in what you said this morning," said Andrew emphatically. "Simon Peter and I have decided that we must settle right now before we get to Jerusalem who should have first place among us."

"We should talk to the Master about it," said James.

"No," answered John. "This is our affair. We must settle it among ourselves. Simon Peter was the first one Jesus asked to give up his fishing and follow him; he should be the leader."

"I think so too," agreed Andrew heartily. Peter kept his thoughts to himself. After all, why should Judas be the chief person? He was not even a Galilean!

"I am going to talk to the others," declared James, hastening ahead. Judas and the Zealot were walking ahead with Jesus.

"Listen!" said James to the disciples. "Do you realize that those two men are going to try to push us out when we get to Jerusalem? We shall not have any place in the new Kingdom at all, unless we protect our rights!"

"We think the best way is to decide now who should be first," said John, continuing. The others nodded vigorous agreement. "I think Simon Peter is the one who should be our leader! After all, the Master chose him first."

Silence settled over the men. James could not understand what was the matter. Finally Philip said hesitantly, "We thought Levi might know how to deal with the Romans."

"Oh, I don't think so!" exclaimed John. "He knows only the Romans in Galilee."

"Besides, the best people in Jerusalem might hold it against him that he was a taxgatherer," added James, without thinking how his words sounded.

Levi flared up. "Well, I am not so sure they will like a fish peddler any better," he remarked bitingly.

"That is beside the point," snapped James. "Simon Peter was the first—and you have to admit it!"

At that moment the Zealot and Judas joined the group. "What are you talking about?" demanded the Zealot. When no one replied, Judas laughed and remarked: "It's not hard to guess! Well, we shall see who is greatest when we get to Jerusalem!"

It was a long and hot trip from Caesarea Philippi to Capernaum, and the men did not stop arguing until they came to the very door of Peter's house. Their home-coming was spoiled. Everyone was in bad humor. Peter remembered how he had longed to see his wife and children when he had looked down on the Lake of Galilee from Mount Hermon. Now this bitter dispute had completely taken away the pleasure of it. Peter's wife could not understand why all the men, even her husband, ate supper in silence. After they had finished eating, James rose and stood in the open doorway, blocking it. He glared angrily at Judas and the Zealot.

He could hardly restrain his bitter resentment against these men, and he was determined to make the Master put them in their place.

But it was Jesus who spoke first—before James could begin his angry accusations. "What were you wrangling about on the road?"

James felt his anger turn against the Master, who was sitting near the door. He had not been wrangling! It was a matter of simple fairness!

"Why were you wrangling on the road today?" Not one of the disciples ventured to answer—the question was put to them a second time.

"An evil spirit of envy and dispute has come among us," said Jesus. The men sensed how deeply hurt he was.

"If any of you wish to be first in the Kingdom of God, you must learn to serve rather than to rule." While he was speaking, Peter's little daughter peeked around the edge of the doorway. She drew back at the sight of the men, but she was so curious that soon she put her head around the corner again. Jesus saw the disciples smile and he turned. "Come here, little girl," he said gently and held out his hands, smiling. She came to him, and he lifted her to his lap. She leaned trustingly against his shoulder and looked shyly at the men.

With his arms around her, Jesus said, "If you are willing to serve even this little child, then you have discovered what it means to be my disciples. But if you do anything to keep even the most despised person from believing in me, you would be better off in the bottom of the sea with a great stone tied around your neck!"

When James finally spoke, his tone was controlled. "But, Master, who is to rule in the new Kingdom when we get to Jerusalem?"

The disciples leaned forward. *Now we shall get this business settled!* thought the Zealot.

"Among the gentiles, a man is great if he rules over many people," answered Jesus. "But in the Kingdom of Heaven it is the other way around: you are great if you serve, not rule."

"But when we get to Jerusalem, Master, who is going to run the new government?" insisted James boldly.

"Do you think of nothing but ruling others? You do not understand my Kingdom at all." Then, slowly and emphatically, Jesus said: "James, if you want to be great in my Kingdom, you must be a servant! If you want to be the chief disciple, you must make yourself the slave of all the others! I myself did not come to rule over many nations—I came to serve the people—yes, even to give my life to buy them from slavery!"

"Master, we know that the new Kingdom will be different," interrupted Peter. "But we shall rule the gentiles, shan't we?" He did not wait for an answer. "You ought to decide which one of us will have the main authority."

The Zealot looked at Peter suspiciously. *So that's how he thinks he will get his way!* he thought. "Now look," he said to Jesus in his most practical tone. "I know many people in Jerusalem who can help us . . ."

James's anger boiled over. "Master, he is interested only in special privileges!"

"That is a lie!" snapped the Zealot, looking fiercely at James. "I want only . . ." Peter's little girl was crying. Harsh voices and frowning faces had frightened her. She clutched Jesus' robe with both tiny hands and buried her head in his robe.

"Here, let me take her," said Peter, starting to rise. But the little girl clung all the closer to Jesus.

"Except you become as little children," said Jesus, "you cannot enter the Kingdom of Heaven." He stood up, holding the child in his arms; he did not intend to listen to the angry debate any longer. "I have appointed you to proclaim the news of the Kingdom of God," he declared. "You are the salt which must season the whole earth. Everything depends on you. But what if the salt loses its taste?" The men again felt in his voice the deep grief they had caused him. "It is fit only to be thrown out and trampled on! Let there be peace between you!"

Jesus gently put Peter's daughter in her father's arms and left the room. He walked down to the shore of the lake. The trip from Caesarea Philippi had been tiring, and he longed to be alone. Under the tiny white stars he was far from the jealousies and selfishness of his followers. Sometimes they were truly noble and brave. They were loyal too, and yet . . . they seemed never to understand! In the quiet night Jesus gave thanks to his Father in heaven for the men who had given up everything to follow him; he prayed that they might soon understand the true meaning of the Kingdom of God.

Suddenly there were running footsteps behind him. Jesus stopped abruptly. Had Herod already discovered that he was back in Galilee? Had spies followed him here so that they could arrest him secretly? Two figures emerged from the darkness.

"Master!" It was John. James was with him. Relief flooded through Jesus.

"We wanted to tell you about something we did." There was a note of pride in John's voice. "Do you remember when James and I went to buy food today? We found a man casting out evil spirits in your name. We put a stop to it right away!"

"We will never allow anyone to interfere with us," added James. "He might even persuade some people to follow him. We want nothing like that!"

Jesus did not answer, but continued to look out over the dark lake. Why had these men followed him all the way out here to tell him this? Were they trying to convince him they were loyal in spite of the day's dispute? Or were they trying to persuade him to do what they wanted? Jesus turned to them. "What made you do a thing like that?" he demanded. "Don't you know that we are trying to give the power of God to everyone who will believe—we are not trying to keep it to ourselves!"

"But he was not one of us," explained James, amazed.

"That makes no difference," answered Jesus. "Are we jealous of his power? Do we think always of our own reputation?"

"But doesn't it make any difference who has power in our Kingdom?" asked James, dumfounded.

"We don't even know the man!" exclaimed John.

"Do not forbid him," replied Jesus. "No one who does a mighty work in my name will be able soon after to speak evil of me. For he that is not against us is for us. If a person so much as gives you a cup of water in my name, God remembers him for it!" His voice was now calm, with the note of sorrow which the men had heard twice before on this day.

"Do you still not understand what is going to happen in Jerusalem?" he said. "I have told you already that I shall be killed! I am not going to Jerusalem to seek the praise of men, but to give up my life for the sake of all men. I shall be betrayed into the power of the high priests. They will hand me over to the Romans to be killed!"

"Master!" cried James desperately. "Do not say such a thing!" Fear chilled him, and the very night seemed to threaten. James had been fighting this thought ever since Jesus had first mentioned his death. "That can never, never happen!"

"In spite of all I have said, you still understand little of my work," said Jesus and left the two men. They did not try to follow, but stood listening to the sound of his footsteps dying away. Then they turned back. There could be no mistaking his meaning this time: the Master knew he would die in Jerusalem.

13. THE MESSIAH MUST DIE

THE next day, Jesus left Capernaum with the Twelve, traveling swiftly on the main highway toward Tiberias, Jericho, and Jerusalem. Early in the afternoon, a wind rose from the south. The sky grew dark; clouds scudded overhead as the disciples plodded along the dusty road. The Lake of Galilee lay to their left. When the sun shone it was refreshing, blue and cool. Now the water was gray, whipped into angry waves by the wind. Only a few months before, the men had nearly drowned in a gale like this.

To their right were bleak hills, bare of trees. An anxious shepherd was driving his sheep to shelter. The black, windy sky reminded the disciples of all the fears that filled them: fear of their own future and distrust of one another.

"Where can we stay for the night, Master?" asked Andrew, raising his voice above a gust that snatched the words from his lips.

Jesus glanced at the sky. "Perhaps we can find an inn at Tiberias."

The wind was hot and laden with dust. Its choking heat kept their skin dry even though the men perspired freely. They covered their faces with their robes to avoid breathing dust.

The air was thick; they could not see the sun, though it was fully four hours before sunset. They could not even see the crest of the ridge rising above them to the right.

"If the wind changes to the southwest, this is sure to turn to rain," remarked James, almost shouting. John nodded. A moment later they heard Andrew call to them.

"Look there!" he shouted. "Up the hill." He was pointing to a tumble-down shed a few yards from the road to their right.

Greatly relieved, the whole group left the road and in a moment were inside the shelter. "We are lucky to find this," said James, throwing the cover off his face. "It is getting cooler, and the wind is changing."

The disciples had hardly caught their breath when they heard a familiar sound. "Sheep!" exclaimed Philip. An instant later a tightly packed flock of frightened sheep crowded into the shed. It overflowed in a moment, but the bleating animals kept on pushing in. Suddenly their shepherd stood in the midst of the men.

"Oh!" He was completely surprised at finding people in his shed.

"We were looking for shelter from the wind and rain," explained Peter.

"Oh . . . why yes!" replied the man. He was embarrassed in the presence of all these strangers. "This is a very poor old shed," he said, smiling apologetically. Shyly he turned away from the disciples and began to count his sheep.

The men watched. He was very slow and started over again three times. They smiled at each other as though to say, "A simple fellow, isn't he?"

The flimsy little shelter rocked under the gusts of the gale, now at its height. The shepherd was too busy counting to notice. Suddenly he jerked up straight. "There is one missing!" Before the disciples could stop him, he plunged into the windy darkness.

"Come back!" shouted James.

"One is missing!" A heavy gust almost drowned the shepherd's reply.

"You'll get hurt!" The man was gone. "How can he ever find

his way?" protested James to the others. "There are gullies and high rocks! He will be killed in the dark!"

"He has practically all the sheep in," declared John. "He could wait a little while till this lets up."

"He would leave his flock here and search all night for a sheep," remarked Jesus.

"He ought not to risk his life like that," answered James.

"A good shepherd is ready to face death to find just one sheep," said Jesus.

Death! The twelve men had been able to think of nothing but fear and death the whole day through. Why did the Master talk about it so much?

At that instant the shepherd came back. Under his arm was a lamb, frightened but not harmed. "There," sighed the man, putting it gently down. "Now all are safe."

"You are hurt!" exclaimed Peter. He knelt and gently touched the man's ankle. The shepherd flinched, but said, "Oh, it is nothing!"

"Let me bandage it," insisted Peter. The man sat down; he was in pain. "How did this happen?" asked Peter, tearing a strip of cloth from the long loose shirt he wore.

"I heard the little one crying and ran toward him," answered the man. "I must have stumbled on a sharp rock."

Jesus was watching the man. "You are a faithful shepherd," he said.

The shepherd looked up quickly and smiled. This man understood! But the disciples were quiet. They knew Jesus was thinking about his own work in Jerusalem.

The wind had veered around and now blew from the southwest. Spattering drops turned into a steady, cold, driving rainstorm.

"Perhaps it will settle the dust," said Andrew hopefully. He was thinking how dejected the sheep looked that had not found room in the shed when he felt cold water on his back. "This place leaks!" he exclaimed. Soon all the men were moving uncomfortably about, trying to find places to stand where they could keep dry. But it was hopeless. The rain poured through the cracks in the old roof.

"We might as well be walking outside as standing here," declared the Zealot in disgust. The suggestion seemed sensible.

"Thank you for the shelter," said Jesus to the shepherd.

The rain had not let up at all, but the men plunged into the night. "Be careful of that ankle," said Peter, the last to go. The shepherd smiled in farewell.

Two hours later the company of miserable disciples arrived in Tiberias. For an hour and a half they had been soaked to the skin. The wind had become quite cold, and they were chilled through. Only after they entered the city of Tiberias did they find an inn where there was room for them.

"This city is crowded with people going to Jerusalem for the feast," observed James, as the disciples stripped off their wet clothing.

"I wonder how Herod likes to have his home city full of loyal Jews," replied John.

"I just hope he does not find out we are here."

The disciples were alarmed when Jesus insisted on teaching the next day in the market place, where people gathered to gossip and buy food.

"What if the tyrant discovers that we are here?" inquired Andrew fearfully. "He could throw us into prison before we could escape!"

"This is an important city for us," replied Jesus. "We must tell the news of the Kingdom to all these pilgrims who are traveling to Jerusalem." Nervously the disciples kept watch for the Roman police while Jesus talked to the people.

It was well that they did. "Here come some Pharisees," warned John. The men were stepping around carts piled with food, taking care to avoid the heavily burdened donkeys that crowded the street. The people dropped back to let them pass. The two Pharisees smiled as they came up to Jesus.

"They seem friendly!" said John, astonished.

"Don't let them deceive you," warned the Zealot.

Jesus received the men graciously. The first said: "Rabbi, we have come to warn you. You had better get out of Tiberias as soon as possible. We have private information from Herod's court that he intends to kill you!"

The disciples were alarmed. The Zealot was frowning and looking at the Pharisees very suspiciously. "Why do you tell us this?" he asked bluntly. They ignored his question, waiting to see what Jesus would say.

Jesus' answer was stern: "Go tell that sly fox that he does not have the power to stop my work!" The people were startled. How did he dare speak like this about the king? "Now I am preaching the good news of the Kingdom of Heaven and helping people," continued Jesus. "When I finish this work I will leave— but I will go to Jerusalem only when the time comes for me to be delivered up to death!"

"Unless you leave Tiberias at once, you will certainly die here," said the second Pharisee.

"No." There was bitter humor in Jesus' tone. "It would hardly be right for a prophet to be killed anywhere but in Jerusalem. It is always our holy city that kills the messengers whom God sends!"

The Pharisees turned and walked away. "Well!" exclaimed John. "For men who want to save us from Herod they certainly act oddly."

"They care nothing about our lives," said the Zealot sourly. "They are just trying to scare us out of Galilee. Herod knows he cannot put us into prison—there would be a riot!"

The people were indeed very loyal to Jesus. Many who had listened to him in their home villages greeted him with great joy when they found him teaching in Tiberias and refused to go on without him.

"We want you to lead us to Jerusalem," declared one man from Capernaum who had often listened to Jesus at the lakeside.

"I must stay here several days to teach others who travel through," answered Jesus.

"Then we shall wait." More and more people joined this man in asking Jesus to lead them to Jerusalem.

The disciples were greatly worried by this. "Herod is sure to hear of this!" exclaimed Andrew, anxiously watching the people crowd around Jesus.

"He must know we are here by now," said John. Any moment

the men expected the officers of King Herod to come to arrest them. They were greatly relieved when Jesus led a small group of especially loyal followers into the hills west of Tiberias.

"At least we are safe out here," observed John as they climbed the brown hill above Herod's capital city. When Jesus stopped, they could see the whole Lake of Galilee spread below them. High above the city rose the towers of Herod's palace. Peter looked northward to where Capernaum lay. Beyond the city he could see Mount Hermon, majestic and cool. A few days before, he had stood on its slopes and gazed at Capernaum, where his wife and children lived. Then he had expected to see them soon. But now he knew he might never see them again.

A ridge concealed the group with Jesus from the road which led west from Tiberias to the Mediterranean Sea. "Tonight we shall rest in the hills," said Jesus to them; there were about seventy beside the disciples. "Tomorrow I will send you to prepare my way to Jerusalem."

The thought of leaving Herod's territory cheered the disciples, but they had not heard all that their Master had to say. "For a few more days I am going to remain here to summon these people to repent and confess that God is King," continued Jesus. "You are to stay with me. I am sending these others into the cities that I will visit." He turned to the Seventy: "Declare the good news of the rule of God. Tell them that the Kingdom is here. Return to me on the third day. Then we shall set out for Jerusalem!"

The people began to talk excitedly with one another. "You must go two by two," continued Jesus, raising his voice. "You have a great work to do, and now is the time to do it! Pray, therefore, that you will find many who will believe your message of the Kingdom of God and help you. Do not let anyone stop you, but press on to tell the gospel in every city where Jews live. You will be in danger; I send you out like sheep among wolves. Just the same, have courage, for you carry good news. Preach this message: 'The rule of God is here; give yourselves to him'!"

After the Seventy had gone, great crowds continued to throng Jesus as he preached in the market place of Tiberias. The anx-

iety that the disciples first felt when Jesus decided to await the
return of the Seventy gradually gave way to optimism when they
saw the great popularity of Jesus.

"The king knows he cannot arrest us," said the Zealot. "Look
at this crowd!"

"It will not be long before we are in Jerusalem!" said John.
Jerusalem! The disciples began to talk eagerly about the new
kingdom.

"Nothing must stop us!" declared James and John. When
the Seventy returned, they were enthusiastic.

"Everyone listened to us!" declared the first two men to return. "People brought their sick to us. They believed our teaching! Even the demons obeyed us!"

"Here is a man who wants to become a follower," said his
companion.

A third person stepped up to Jesus and said very sincerely, "I
will go with you anywhere."

Jesus looked at him keenly and said: "My way is not easy.
The foxes in the woods have holes to sleep in. Even the wild
birds have nests—but I have no home and no place to give you."

"I will follow you anywhere," said the man again.

Through the day others returned. Every hour the disciples
heard good reports of the success of the Seventy. At sunset all
the followers whom Jesus had sent out gathered in the hills.
The bright rays of the sinking sun lighted Jesus' face as he
raised his hand to quiet the excited men.

"Satan is utterly defeated!" he declared. "The power of God
is yours! Nothing can stand in the way of God's rule!" The
people could not restrain their excitement. They burst into a
babble of conversation. One man cried out, "Master, we even
have power over demons!"

Jesus answered quickly. "You should rejoice because you know
what it is to be a part of God's Kingdom—not because you can
do miracles!" He raised his arms to pray. Like the silent shadow
that had stolen over them as the sun sank from sight, a reverent
hush settled over the crowd.

"Father in heaven, I thank thee that thou hast concealed thy-
self from men who think they are wise. I praise thee that thou

hast revealed all these things to the humble and the simple. I praise thee that it is thy purpose to rule over all who are willing to give their hearts to thee."

While the group were returning to their lodging in Tiberias, James and John made a discovery that shocked and angered them. One of the Seventy had been turned roughly away from a town on the border of Samaria. Indignantly the two fishermen came with the man to Jesus.

"This man was driven out of a village in Samaria," they said angrily. "Let us call down fire from the sky and burn up these people!"

"No!" commanded Jesus. "We have not come to destroy men's lives but to save them."

"Why should these worthless Samaritans be allowed to stand in the way of the Kingdom of God?" demanded James hotly. "We should destroy them. They are enemies of God!"

"Our own towns in Galilee have rejected us as harshly as any town in Samaria," answered Jesus. He pointed northward toward the villages on the Lake of Galilee. His voice sent a chill through the fishermen: "O Bethsaida, you are doomed—you are doomed! If my miracles had been done in Tyre or Sidon, they would have repented long ago. But you have turned your back on me! And you, Capernaum! Will you become great? No! You shall be utterly destroyed for your sin!"

These towns—the ones James and John knew and loved the best—Jesus condemned because they had not accepted his gospel! Did he believe Galilee had rejected him? Of what mighty destruction was he speaking?

By morning the fishermen had forgotten Jesus' somber warning. The little waves on the lake sparkled in the brightness of the sun. As Jesus' followers walked briskly with him along the road toward Jerusalem, they could talk of nothing but their arrival in the holy city.

"We shall be welcomed in Jerusalem," said Peter. "See how well liked the Master is by all the pilgrims!"

"That is true," agreed a man from Capernaum. "But just the same, Pilate is a dangerous man. Did you hear what he did at the last festival?"

"No," answered James. "What was that?"

"Some Zealots from Galilee started a riot in the Temple. I did not see what happened myself, but they say that the Roman soldiers put a stop to the trouble and within a few hours Pilate crucified twelve of the Zealots." He looked at the others. "There were many Galileans in Jerusalem—but that did not stop Pilate!"

"But we are not going to start a riot," James hastened to say. "As Judas says, we will work from the inside until the right time." Peter glanced curiously at the other men. No doubt of the future seemed to cross their minds. Peter restrained a desire to interrupt. Finally James turned to him and asked, "Do you think Jesus would let himself be trapped by the officials?"

Very forcefully Peter answered: "I do not think he will be trapped. I do not know what will happen. But do not forget what he said; again and again he has told us that he will be killed in Jerusalem!"

"Oh, I am sure he doesn't mean it the way it sounds," said James hastily. "He was discouraged when he said that."

"Just the same, he definitely said his work in Jerusalem would cost his life!"

"There will be no new kingdom for any of us if that happens!" replied James.

14. A DAY OF VICTORY

WITHIN two hours Jesus and his friends had reached the southern end of the Lake of Galilee. They knew that the heavy rain had made the lake rise almost to the point of flooding the water front at Tiberias. But they never expected the sight that lay before them.

Usually the Jordan wound sluggishly between low banks. Now a huge overflow was pouring out of the lake, filling the wide river bed with muddy water. The disciples looked with dismay at the uprooted bushes and broken limbs swirling past them. They could hardly believe that this destructive flood had been the narrow Jordan they had forded so many times before.

"Do you think that we can find a place to wade through?" James and John were walking down the bank.

James shook his head. "It is not deep, but it is terribly swift. Look how wide it is!" A quarter mile of water lay between them and the other side.

"I guess we shall have to travel down the road on this side." They turned back to the others.

"I am not going through Samaria!" exclaimed James.

"Perhaps we can find a shallow place to cross before we get that far," replied John.

None of the other people were willing to risk their lives by attempting to ford the rushing river. "Come!" called Jesus to the ones who stood wondering what to do. He started down the road toward Samaria; some of the people looked doubtful, but no one objected. The road followed the high hills that shut in the Jordan Valley on the west, but it was well above the flood level of the river. Fully four miles to the east stretched the broad lowlands of the Jordan, small hills, an occasional steep bluff, and at the center, the flooded river.

As the group traveled south, the flat valley narrowed and the hills came closer on both east and west. Some of the farms near the river were under water. "We may be able to cross near here," observed Andrew. They had walked about five miles. "Do you remember if there is a bridge on the road across to Gadara?"

James pointed to a white strip below them. "The road is just ahead."

Jesus walked past the crossroad without turning. "Surely he is not going through Samaria!" exclaimed James.

"Has he forgotten how these people treated our messengers?" asked John.

"Perhaps he does not want all the travelers on the other road to know he is going to the Passover," guessed one man. "He is a complete stranger to the people in this part of Samaria. We could go all the way through the province before anyone would discover we are on our way to Jerusalem."

"Perhaps we shall find lodging more easily along this road," observed another.

"I doubt if anyone will even sell us food," said James pessimistically. "Samaritans are mean."

"We shall soon find out," remarked Andrew. "This road leads right to Scythopolis."

This town was just over the border from Galilee. It was the largest of the ten cities which together were called "Decapolis"; it was part of ancient Samaria, and Jews usually avoided it. North of the city the Jordan Valley grew suddenly wide; here the range of high hills along which they were walking turned almost due west.

"Perhaps there will be some here who know the Master is a great prophet," said one of the men hopefully as the city came into view.

"Probably never even heard of him," replied another. At that moment a small group of men came out of a ramshackly house standing just outside the city gate. Some hobbled; one crawled on his knees.

"Lepers!" exclaimed John. "Don't get near them!" The ten sick men came straight toward Jesus. Everyone sighed with relief when they stopped several paces from the band of Galileans.

"Unclean! We are unclean!" they called. The law compelled them to warn everyone of their disease with this cry. "Master, have mercy upon us."

They were indeed a pitiable sight. With inward pain, Jesus looked at their wasted bodies, mere skin and bone. Repulsive scars from the disease marked their faces.

"These men seem to know the Master," murmured Andrew in surprise.

"They might be Galileans," replied James. "Perhaps they live here because they were driven out of their homes." The people were afraid that the lepers might come near them, but the twelve disciples knew that Jesus intended to help them.

"Make ready and go immediately to Jerusalem," commanded Jesus. "Go to the priest there and get a certificate showing that you are clean according to the Law of Moses." The ten men turned without a word and made for the leper house. In a moment they were out again, taking the road around the outside of the city. On the way to Jerusalem they would beg food.

"Let us go into the city," said Jesus. He had hardly come into the shadow of the high wall when one of the lepers came running back. He threw himself down in front of Jesus and cried out: "Blessed art thou, Master! God is good! I am clean!" It was true. The men could see no sign of the terrible disease.

"Where are the other nine? asked Jesus. "Were they not healed also?"

"This man is not from Galilee!" exclaimed Andrew under his breath.

"Is this Samaritan the only one to come back and thank me?" Jesus asked the people. He turned to the man. "Get up and go back to your own home. Your faith has made you well."

The gate into Scythopolis was like a dark tunnel because the wall was so thick. Roman guards stationed on the inside examined the travelers as they passed through. If they were surprised to find a large group of Galileans in a town on the border of Samaria, they said nothing.

"This town seems different from the one that refused us," admitted James. Every one of the people who accompanied Jesus found a place to stay. They discovered that many of the townsmen knew about Jesus. Some even gathered curiously in the courtyard of the inn where Jesus rested. By the time they left Scythopolis the next morning everyone knew they were there.

"The Master could make many disciples here," observed Andrew enthusiastically.

All the followers of Jesus were in high spirits. Even though Jesus kept a fast pace, they did not fall behind. At noon they passed through a large town, but Jesus paused only long enough for them to draw water to drink. Farther south they entered the narrowest part of the Jordan Valley. The road followed the brink of low limestone cliffs which overhung the Jordan. The swift water was cutting into the banks; whirlpools and rapids swirled below them. Occasionally they had to walk around places where the river had undermined a section of the bank and caused a cave-in.

Even though the river constantly washed away portions of their farms, the people raised heavy crops. The farmers lived in crowded villages along the road. Between the wheat from the rich soil and the sheep that grazed on the hills above, the people were quite prosperous.

For two days Jesus pressed forward without a rest. As the group approached the borders of Judea, the valley gradually widened until the mountains across the river were blue in the haze that hung heavy in the air. The damp heat had nearly exhausted the travelers, but some inward force seemed to drive Jesus faster every hour. In the afternoon of the second day they crossed the first of the streams that flowed from the highlands behind Jericho. Ahead of the disciples, clear to the foot of the distant hills, lay green fields of wheat, fig orchards, and vineyards. Beside the road were rows of stately palms.

"There is Jericho!" Everyone looked ahead. The city stood on a low, flat hill. Its walls rose high above the trees. The Galileans could see very clearly the beautiful theater built thirty years before by Herod the Great, father of Herod Antipas, ruler of Galilee. Beside it stood the massive fortress which he had built to defend Jericho. Dominating both city and plain stood the square stone tower of Cyprus; from this high lookout Herod's soldiers could easily see any enemy who might dare attack Jericho.

Jewish pilgrims crowded the road. "They must have waded the Jordan at the ford where we first heard John the Baptizer," commented Andrew to John.

"The way we came is shorter," answered John, thinking of the many loads of salted fish he and Andrew had brought to Jerusalem on the road east of the river. The disciples saw the Galilean pilgrims on the road staring at Jesus and murmuring to one another. At length one man came up to John.

"Wasn't your Rabbi in Tiberias a few days ago?" he asked. John nodded. The man and his friends joined the group with Jesus. Others followed.

"This is not good," observed Andrew.

"It certainly would be better not to cause any disturbance in Jericho," agreed Peter.

"We shall be in serious trouble if Pilate's local commander sends him word that we caused a riot here," added Judas. "I hope these people keep their heads."

Outside the gate of Jericho sat the usual line of beggars, ragged, filthy, and diseased. Some were silent, but others called

out, asking alms. Hardly anyone paid any attention. Suddenly
there was a loud cry from the side of the road.

"Jesus! Jesus! Thou Son of David! Messiah! Have mercy on
me!"

"Shut up!" snapped someone. Others looked harshly at the
beggar who had shouted, but he could not see their hard faces.
He was blind.

"Jesus! Messiah! Have pity on me!" His voice was louder than
before.

"In the name of heaven, make that wretch be quiet!" burst
out Judas. "We shall have the whole Roman army on us if anyone hears him talking as though Jesus were going to lead a
revolution!"

Jesus stopped. "Who is calling to me?"

"Oh, just some beggar," answered James.

"Bring him to me." The man who had scolded the beggar
said to him: "Don't worry. The Master himself is calling you."
The blind man leaped to his feet, threw off his tattered coat,
and pushed his way through the crowd toward Jesus.

"What do you want me to do for you?" asked Jesus.

The beggar dropped to his knees. "O Master, that I might
be able to see again!"

A hush had fallen over the crowd. Jesus said: "Open your
eyes. Your faith has made you well again." The man looked
around him. He saw the people, the city wall above him, the
palm trees at the side of the road. Jesus turned and led the
crowd through the gate into Jericho. People clustered around
the beggar as he walked after Jesus. He talked loudly and hap-
pily, hardly able to express his joy.

Judas came up to Jesus. "Can't we send that man away? Think
what will happen if the Romans hear him babbling like this!"

"Let him tell what has happened to him," answered Jesus.
"We have come to Judea to proclaim the gospel. That
man has found the Kingdom of Heaven. Let him declare it to
everyone!"

"We are losing our chance to win over the high priests in Jerusalem!" burst out Judas. "Before tomorrow night word will

reach them that the people are trying to make Jesus king! They will all be against us!"

"Well, there is nothing to do about it now," said the Zealot. The man in front of Judas stopped in his tracks and Judas ran into him. "What is the matter now?" he demanded impatiently.

The Zealot pointed to a tree over their heads. "Look!" A man was standing on a heavy lower limb of one of the sycamore trees that grew at the side of the street. The whole crowd gaped. Jesus spoke with someone in the crowd for a moment and then called to the man in the tree: "Zacchaeus, come down here! I want to visit your home."

Judas turned to a man beside him. "Who is that fellow?"

"He is the chief tax collector in Jericho. He is very rich."

"A tax collector!" exploded Judas. He turned to the Zealot. "Did you hear that? He wants to stay with a tax collector! Why does he insist on mixing with such people? Everyone will say he is a lover of traitors and sinners!" If Judas had not known it was useless, he would have protested to Jesus then and there.

Zacchaeus climbed out of the tree and stood in front of Jesus. "May I come to your home?" asked Jesus again.

"Oh, yes, Master!" exclaimed Zacchaeus, and he turned to lead the way.

The rumor spread fast. The Galilean Prophet was staying with Zacchaeus! The deliverer of Israel—staying with a tax collector? Impossible! Perhaps he was not Messiah at all!

The publican knew that people considered him a traitor. He knew how much it meant that Jesus had chosen him for a friend. The next morning, just before Jesus left his home, Zacchaeus declared in the presence of all the disciples: "I am not the man I was yesterday. I intend to be a different person. If I have cheated anyone in collecting taxes, I will give half of all that I possess to the poor; and I will give every man whom I cheated four times what I took from him."

Jesus smiled. "Zacchaeus, this day God has forgiven your sin and accepted you in his Kingdom. Because you believe, you are a true son of Abraham."

After they had left, Judas could contain himself no longer.

"Master, think of our task in Jerusalem!" he exclaimed. "What will the best people think of us? They will never believe we come to do God's will if we act as though we approved of law-breakers!"

"Judas," answered Jesus, "the Son of Man has come to seek and to save those who are lost. Zacchaeus was waiting for some-. one to summon him to repent and submit himself to God. My Father has sent me into the world to tell just such people—outcasts, beggars, sinners, even gentiles—that he is ready to receive anyone who will repent."

Many people were waiting at the city gate for Jesus to lead them to Jerusalem. Going before them, he walked from the fertile lowlands around Jericho into the bleak hills of Judea. Above the city the travelers paused for a last look. Beyond the green plain lay the river, hidden in a tangle of trees, bushes, and high grass. Wise travelers crossed the river only at the regular fords because this jungle concealed wolves, jackals, bears, and lions even this far south. The Dead Sea lay perfectly still. Mud flats marked the place where the Jordan emptied into it.

Andrew was glad that they traveled in a large group, for this steep road was a favorite of robbers. In Galilee they often heard reports of travelers being ambushed, beaten, and robbed in these lonely mountains. In small knots the disciples argued about the outcome of the things that had happened in Jericho. By the time they had covered the fifteen rough miles to the outskirts of Jerusalem, the men were more deeply excited than they themselves realized. All their hope and faith in the Master was to be put to the test! Drawing near the holy city, the road crossed the southern shoulder of the Hill of Olives and here the men first caught sight of the capital city of Palestine. There were many beautiful buildings; Pilate had just built a graceful new aqueduct through the mountains to Jerusalem. The little town of Bethphage lay outside the city wall. But the disciples had eyes only for Mount Zion and the Temple. They never saw Jerusalem without a thrill. The Temple was the symbol of their religious faith, the place where God had established his glory. Mount Zion held the eye of every traveler who ascended to the gates of the holy city.

Jesus called two of the disciples. "We will wait here at the Hill of Olives," he said. "You go into Bethphage. Just after you enter the town you will see a colt which has never been ridden tied to a post beside the door of a house. Bring it to me. If anyone asks you what right you have to do it, tell him, 'The Lord needs it, and he will send it back immediately.'"

On the way to Bethphage one of the men said, "Did you know the Master had planned to ride into Jerusalem on a donkey?"

"No," answered his companion. Both men were surprised to find that Jesus had prepared for his visit. When they got back to the Hill of Olives, several men took off their cloaks and placed them on the back of the colt. Jesus seated himself on the animal, and the entire group moved toward the gate of Jerusalem.

Pilgrims who crowded the roads stopped to watch, then recognized Jesus and joined the crowd. Excitement became intense. When the gate of the holy city came into view, several men ran ahead to clear the way. Snatches of song and psalms of praise could be heard on every side. The tremendous enthusiasm of the people did not break out, however, until the procession entered the city.

For a moment all was quiet as they walked under the cool shadowed gate. Then the colt carried Jesus out of the gate into the city. It seemed to the amazed disciples that a thousand people filled the cobblestone street.

"Hosanna! Save us now!" cried the crowd. "Blessed is the one who comes in the name of the Lord God. Blessed is the messenger whom God has sent to deliver his people! Hosanna! Hosanna!"

"Pilate will hear about this within an hour!" shouted Judas in the ear of the Zealot.

"Nonsense! There is nothing to fear. Look at this crowd! Pilate would never dare arrest us!"

Judas rushed up to Jesus and pulled at his robe. "Master, make them stop! Make them stop!"

Jesus' answer cut through the tumult. "If these people did not proclaim the Kingdom, the very stones in the street would have to cry out!"

Men were taking off their cloaks and throwing them in the

street in front of Jesus. Palm branches which people had brought from Jericho were scattered before Jesus as though he were a king advancing to his throne on a royal carpet.

"Blessed is the kingdom of our great King David!" shouted the people. "Blessed is his Son who comes to deliver us!" As Jesus rode by, everyone fell into step behind him, singing and shouting praises. Jesus led the crowd up the hill of Zion straight to the Temple. He got off the colt and entered. Hundreds pushed in after him, still shouting hosannas.

What Jesus saw shocked him. It was early evening, and most of the people who came to sacrifice had left. But the courtyard of the house of God was neither empty nor quiet. A large number of young bulls and sheep were tethered there and made a great disturbance. Jesus had seen these animals here when he had visited Jerusalem before; indignation rose up inside him. Priests were carrying water to the bullocks. Others were putting away small tables where they counted money as they sold the animals. The whole scene reminded Jesus more of a barnyard or a market place than the Temple of God.

With rising anger, Jesus walked slowly around the entire courtyard. He examined everything in it very closely. The people saw his frown, and their enthusiasm melted away. The shouting stopped.

"What is he going to do?" murmured Andrew. Jesus turned his back on the whole disgusting scene and walked out of the Temple.

"Why has he gone?" everyone asked. Only the disciples followed Jesus. The people scattered to the places where they lodged, wondering what would happen on the morrow.

"Why was he angry?" asked Andrew.

"I don't know," answered Peter.

"There are many things I should like to know," observed Judas.

There was deep feeling in Peter's voice when he spoke again. "There is one thing certain: very soon we shall know when he intends to bring in the new Kingdom. The people are for us. Perhaps tomorrow will tell!"

15. DISPUTE IN THE TEMPLE

Dusk on the Hill of Olives was quiet and restful after the excitement of the day. The gentle wind in the olive trees, which grew thickly in the Garden of Gethsemane, was so different from the noise and smell of the Temple courtyard!

While the disciples slept, Jesus went deeper into the Garden, where he could pray alone. When he knelt on the rocky ground, the moon, almost full, was just rising in the east. But when Jesus finally returned to the Twelve and wrapped his coat around him to sleep, the moon was high above, cold and white.

The sound of travelers on the road through the olive orchard awakened Peter the next morning. The morning sunlight threw long shadows on the ground. Between the trees Peter could see pilgrims passing along the road. Jerusalem would be crowded this Passover season! For a moment Peter could not remember why he felt so excited when he awoke. Then the events of the day before flooded into his memory. He stood up stiffly. He had been cold all night; the hard ground was a poor bed for men who would soon be ruling the gentiles! Jesus stood up and stretched.

"Come, my followers!" he called. "There is work to do in the Temple!"

The men arose and walked down the slope to a small spring that trickled from under a rock. When they had washed, Jesus led them to the road that crossed the Kidron Valley toward the Golden Gate of the Temple. All the men were hungry.

Along the road they found no food for sale. Everyone who lived outside the city walls bought food in the market of Jerusalem. Just above the Kidron, a leafy tree stood beside the road.

"It is too early for figs," remarked Andrew. Jesus did not hear: he was gazing at the tree. He turned to the twelve men.

"This tree is a good picture of the religion of the priests. It has many leaves and looks strong. But there is not one bit of fruit on it." He pointed to the Temple above them. The sun shone brilliantly on Mount Zion. It was a sight to inspire every pilgrim who climbed the Jericho road. "The Temple is beautiful. There are many priests. Our Law is righteous. Moses and the Prophets were great teachers. But our religion is all fine appearance! It is producing nothing! Our priests and rulers obey the Romans. The Temple is filled with people who spend their time selling bullocks and exchanging money!"

The disciples realized that Jesus had been deeply offended by the things he had seen in the Temple the evening before. Jesus continued in a quieter tone: "There was once a man who had a fig tree like this one planted in his vineyard. He came to see if it was producing fruit, but there was none to be found. There were no figs the next year either. When he found none the third year, he said to his gardener: 'That tree has not given us any fruit in three years. Cut it down. It is just taking up valuable ground.'

"But the gardener said: 'Let me give it one more chance. Let me dig round it and put manure on it. If it does not bear fruit next year, we will cut it down.'" With great force Jesus said: "Our nation has had more than enough time to show results! God will judge us for failing him! Let this fig tree teach you that God will condemn all religion that does not produce real fruit, no matter how fine it may look!"

Jesus' voice struck dread into the disciples. He sounded like Jeremiah pronouncing doom on the city of Jerusalem. And he had said there was work for him at the Temple! What did he intend to do? As the disciples followed Jesus through the Valley of Kidron, they were uneasy.

Jesus strode through the Golden Gate into the Temple without looking to the right or to the left. He walked through Solomon's Porch into the courtyard. Gentiles were allowed to come this far, but only Jews could go farther. Several gates led through a second wall into another court. Over each gate hung a great sign:

NO FOREIGNER IS ALLOWED

INSIDE THE WALL

SURROUNDING THE SANCTUARY.

WHOEVER IS CAUGHT WILL BE PUT TO DEATH!

HE ALONE WILL BE RESPONSIBLE!

One whole side of the outer yard was filled with stamping bulls and sheep. The bawling of the cattle, the stirring of the nervous sheep, and the fluttering of pigeons in cages piled high on the ground made great confusion. Even this early in the morning dust filled the air over the courtyard.

High above the Temple area rose four stone towers. Andrew shaded his eyes and looked up. Steel armor glinted in the sunlight. From this lookout, called the Tower of Antonia, Pilate's Roman soldiers kept keen watch over everything that happened in the Temple.

But it was not the tethered animals or the bustling crowds that caught Jesus' attention. Not even the Roman fort interested him after the first glance. What grated most disagreeably upon him was the bickering of the priests. Even above the noise the disciples could hear the priests arguing with pilgrims who needed an animal to sacrifice.

Jesus and the Twelve stopped to watch one priest. As they listened, Peter saw his Master's anger rising. A Galilean had brought a young bull all the way from his home. To the disciples he looked like a farmer who did not have much to live on. Such men usually sacrificed a sheep or a pigeon. But this man must have wanted to give a better sacrifice. He was watching the priest examine the legs of his bullock. Finally the priest straightened up.

"No! This beast will not do."

"But I brought this bull all the way from Galilee," protested the farmer.

"I can't help that," answered the priest. "He is not good enough."

"Not good enough!" cried the man in dismay. "That is the best bull I ever raised!"

"All right, then; look!" The priest pointed to a small cut on the rear leg of the bullock.

"But that happened on the trip," explained the farmer. "There is nothing really wrong with him."

"Do you want to offer a sacrifice to God which is not perfect?" The man did not answer. "I'll tell you what I will do," the disciples heard the priest say. "I will trade you a perfect sheep for this bull."

The farmer's face reddened angrily. For an instant he seemed about to strike the priest; then he jerked at the tether and led his bullock out of the Temple court without replying.

Jesus turned to the disciples, his voice indignant. "That man brought the best he had—and was turned away!"

Jesus walked toward the Beautiful Gate, between the outer courtyard and the inner court where the Temple building stood. At the foot of the steps which led through the gate he stopped. On each side of the gate were money-changers. Everyone who wished to give money had to go to the tables where these men sat and buy Jewish coins with their Roman and Greek money. Because there was a profit on this exchange, the Temple treasury had grown rich. Pilate had forced the high priest to use some of this money to pay for the great aqueduct that brought water to Jerusalem.

The men were weighing coins on their scales. Clinking money and noisy arguing made the scene all the more like a public market. Jesus stood before the row of tables, looking at the money-changers. Suddenly he spoke in a voice that was firm and clear. The arguing stopped; men forgot the money and looked up. Silence settled over that part of the Temple courtyard; Jesus had taken command. "It is written in the Scriptures, 'My house shall be called a house of prayer for all the nations!' But you have made it a den of robbers!"

Jesus stepped swiftly toward the first table and with a sweep of his arm threw the table over into the dust. The scales crashed to the ground; money rolled everywhere. In an instant Jesus was striding down the whole row. The money-changers were terrified. Jesus did not leave a single table standing. Scales and coins, records on parchment, and chairs lay in confusion on the ground. The onlookers could hardly believe what they saw; who could this be, who dared clear this courtyard as though it were his own?

Judas moved quickly toward Jesus. "Stop! Stop!" he cried out.

But Jesus paid no attention. He turned to those who were selling animals and pigeons and cried out: "Take these things away! You shall not make my Father's house a house of trade!" He picked up a piece of rope and, knotting a whip of cords, began to drive the bullocks out of the Temple.

People stood as though paralyzed. Heavy swirls of dust hung in the morning air. The empty cages from which the pigeons had escaped lay scattered. Judas stood stock-still behind Jesus, not daring to protest again. The Roman guards peered alertly from the Tower of Antonia, but now all had become quiet below them.

"Come! Let us leave this place!" Jesus walked across the broad royal porch and down toward the market place of Jerusalem.

The disciples finally started after him. "All Jerusalem saw him do it!" exclaimed Andrew.

Judas could hold back no longer. "Why did he have to do a thing like this!" he cried passionately. "This will turn everyone against us!" The other eleven men knew that the Romans had seen it all; within a few minutes it would be reported to Pilate. "The priests will be against us!" burst out Judas again. "What can we do when every important person will say that we are wrong?" Not even the Zealot could find an answer.

The disciples heard rushing footsteps behind them. Fear clutched them as they caught sight of a crowd pouring down the street from the Temple. They gathered around Jesus. "Hosanna! The Son of David has come to rule his eternal kingdom! Save us now!" Through the narrow streets on every side, people came running.

"These people are not against us!" cried the Zealot. Peter caught sight of the man whose bullock had been rejected by the priest. Of course, this man would be on Jesus' side!

Jesus waved his hand, and the crowd gradually became quiet. "The Kingdom of God is present among you!" he said to them. "God rules every man who trusts him. Nothing is impossible for a man who has faith!" For a moment an outburst of hosannas drowned his voice. "God does not desire more offerings and sac- rifices! He wants you to trust him as your Father! He wants you to love his will above everything else and to obey him faithfully. Any man who hears and believes my word shall have eternal life in God's Kingdom!"

Already the crippled, blind, and diseased were pressing for- ward to the place where Jesus stood. Looking at them with pity, Jesus repeated words now familiar to the disciples: "The Spirit of the Lord is upon me, for he has consecrated me to preach the gospel to the poor. He has sent me to proclaim release for cap- tives and recovery of sight for the blind. He has sent me to set free the oppressed and to proclaim this is the year of the Lord's blessing!" It seemed a long time since Peter had heard Jesus read from Isaiah in the synagogue at Nazareth.

"You are the One the Prophets tell about!" cried a beggar in the crowd. "You are the Son of David!"

All day Jesus remained in Jerusalem, teaching and healing. Roman soldiers came to investigate, but they did not disturb him.

"Look at all these people," the Zealot said enthusiastically. "He must be getting ready to declare himself king! He did just the right thing this morning!"

Judas turned on him. "The people cannot make anyone king," he said bluntly. "The Romans and the priests are all that count!" The other disciples wavered between hope and discouragement. Later in the day Pharisees and priests joined the crowd. "See?" said Judas. "Already they are spying on us." The hearts of the Twelve sank. Judas must be right. They urged Jesus to leave Jerusalem immediately, but not until evening did Jesus lead them back to the Hill of Olives.

"At least he is not going to risk being arrested by staying in the city at night," sighed Peter in relief. "The Roman soldiers will never find us here unless someone tells them where we are."

None of the disciples slept soundly that night. Again Jesus spent most of the night in prayer. The men rose early, glad to be rid of the discomfort of the cold ground, but dreading to enter Jerusalem again.

Jesus did not seek the crowds in the market place; he walked straight to the Temple. The money-changers had not come back; no animals stamped their hoofs in the courtyard. James glanced up at the Tower of Antonia. Did the guard know that Jesus was the man who had caused the riot yesterday?

Jesus paid no attention to guards or priests. He sat down near the gate where the Jews entered the inner court to put gifts into the Temple offering box. Within an hour the rumor spread through Jerusalem that he was in the Temple. People began to come in great numbers. Scribes, Pharisees, and Roman soldiers were there too. After Jesus had been teaching awhile one of the scribes interrupted. He lived on the Temple grounds.

"What I want to know," he demanded, "is what right you have to call the Temple of God your Father's house? How do you dare act as you do?"

"I will ask you a question," replied Jesus. "If you answer it, I will tell you what right I have to act as I do. Where did John the Baptizer get his right to preach? From God in heaven, or was he given it by some man, perhaps a priest?"

From God, of course, thought all the people instantly.

The scribe knew what the people believed. He reflected, *If I say, "From heaven," then he will ask us why we did not believe John's word. But if I say, "From men"—no, that will never do! These people all think John came from God!* After a long pause, the scribe said, "I do not know."

"All right, then," said Jesus. "That is why you cannot understand where I get the right to act as I do! Listen to a story I shall tell you. A man planted a vineyard. He put a fence around it, dug a wine press, and built a guard tower to protect it. Then he leased his vineyard to some farmers and went away. At harvest-time he sent a servant to collect the rent, but the farmers beat the man and sent him away with nothing. The owner sent another servant, but the farmers clubbed him on the head and insulted him. The farmers abused every man the owner sent; they even killed some of them. Finally the owner thought, 'I am sure they will respect my son.' So he sent his only son to collect the rent.

"When the wicked farmers saw the young man coming, they said to each other: 'This young fellow will inherit the vineyard. If we kill him, we will possess it!' So they beat the young man to death and threw his body over the fence of the vineyard.

"What will the owner of the vineyard do?" demanded Jesus. "He will utterly destroy these evil farmers and will give the vineyard to other people whom the farmers hated!"

The scribe backed away and went into the inner court. "Look at him!" whispered Judas to Peter. "Do you know what he is going to do? He is going to report to the others!" Judas began to move away.

"Where are you going?" asked Peter.

"I don't want to be seen around here." Peter followed him to the outer gate of the Temple. He was disturbed by what had happened the day before, but he put on a bold manner with Judas.

"I don't think there is any reason to be afraid," remarked Peter.

Judas looked at Peter as though he had no sense at all. "Anyone can see that we haven't a chance. The priests are plotting against us right this minute. Look at that guard," he pointed at the tower; "he sees everything we do!" Peter did not reply. "Anyhow, did you hear that story Jesus told? You heard him say that they killed the son too, didn't you?"

Peter jerked up his head. "Do you mean . . ."

Judas nodded. "All the way from Galilee he has told us that he would be killed here."

Peter looked over at Jesus. "He acts very deliberately. He seems to know what he is doing."

Judas laughed bitterly. "He knows what he is doing, all right!" He caught sight of some Pharisees coming down the steps of the Beautiful Gate. "There are some more!" He turned his face away from them.

Peter started toward Jesus, but Judas hung back. "Don't you want to hear what they say?" asked Peter. "Come on."

"I'm keeping out of sight from now on. And you had better look out for yourself too!" Peter did not wait to argue.

"Rabbi," the Pharisee was saying, "we know you are a sincere and fearless man. You have a reputation for never playing politics. You always tell men to do what God wants." The people were surprised. This Pharisee did not speak in a superior tone like the others. "Tell me, Rabbi," asked the Pharisee, "is it right to pay taxes to the Romans or not?"

Peter knew instantly that it was a trap. If Jesus answered that the Jews should pay the Roman tax, he would be called a traitor to his people. If he said the tax was wrong, he would be reported to Pilate and arrested. A clever trick!

"Why do you try to trap me?" demanded Jesus. "Bring me a Roman coin." He held it up and asked the Pharisee, "Whose picture is stamped on this?"

"Caesar's," he answered.

"All right, then," said Jesus. "Give to the Romans what belongs to them—but be sure that you give to God what belongs to him!"

Jesus had escaped the trap, but Peter was puzzled. What could he mean by saying, "Give to the Romans what belongs to them"? They were not going to live under the Romans much longer!

The people were angry with this attempt to trick Jesus. They murmured threats when another scribe spoke up, "Rabbi, what is the most important command in the Law?"

Jesus replied without hesitating. "The Lord your God is one God and you must love him with your whole heart, your whole soul, your whole mind, and your whole strength. And the second is this: You must love your neighbor as yourself. No commands are greater than these."

"I think you are right, Rabbi," answered the scribe thoughtfully. "It is much more important to love God and one's neighbor sincerely than to make many sacrifices in the Temple."

The disciples were suspicious; what new trick was this? But Jesus answered the scribe warmly. "You are not far from the Kingdom of God!"

Andrew came through the crowd toward Peter. "Have you seen Judas?"

"We were talking just a minute ago." Both the men searched among the people. "He must have gone!" The fishermen were puzzled. "He did not want the officials to see him with us," remarked Peter.

Later in the afternoon the people began to leave the Temple court. The disciples became anxious. With hardly anyone around, the Romans could easily arrest Jesus! In a few more minutes there would be almost no one in the Temple. But still Jesus talked to a few persons who needed him. When they left the men sighed with relief. "Where is Judas?" asked Jesus. Not one of the disciples knew.

Judas had not left the Temple, as Peter supposed. At that very moment he was only a few yards away from them. After talking to Peter, he had walked through the inner court to the council chamber of the high priest. His knock interrupted a secret meeting.

A priest opened the door. "What do you want here?"

"I want to talk with the high priest." Inside he saw the rulers of the Temple.

"Let him in," ordered Caiaphas, the high priest. "You are with the Galilean!" he said accusingly the instant he saw Judas.

"I was, but I am no longer," replied Judas. "Now I know that he is really very dangerous!" The men looked at him suspiciously. Judas plunged ahead, trying to please the hard-faced men. "This Jesus does not really love the Law. He disobeys the great Rabbis! He cannot help us against the Romans. The Kingdom he talks about is a dream! All he does is arouse the people, and I am afraid he will bring Pilate's vengeance upon us all!"

The priests were surprised. The high priest demanded, "Well, what do you want?"

"I will help you take him for thirty silver coins." The dreadful offer was made. He was pale, and beads of sweat stood out on his forehead.

"Will you help us arrest him secretly—so that the people will not find out?" Every eye was on Judas.

"I will."

"Very well, then. It is a bargain."

16. THE END OF HOPE

LATE that night Judas crept into the olive orchard. Silently he lay down among the disciples; but he did not close his eyes. He listened alertly to catch any sound that would tell him that the others were awake. There was only uneasy breathing and restless turning. He lifted his head and looked carefully among the sleepers. Where was Jesus?

Stealthily Judas arose. He knew the ground well; many times he had strolled in this peaceful grove during visits to Jerusalem. He walked through the olive orchard to the road that led to Bethany. Across the Valley of Kidron the walls of Jerusalem gleamed white in the moonlight. Still he saw no sign of Jesus.

Judas did not cross the deserted road, but walked carefully toward the section of the orchard that lay farthest from the

sleeping disciples. A low wall loomed ahead; here the great press
was built which crushed the oil from the olives. Silently Judas
climbed over the wall and stood still for a moment, listening
intently. But Judas heard nothing. He started across the en-
closure around the olive press, but stopped suddenly.

Only a few steps away from Judas knelt Jesus, his face bowed
almost to the ground. The moonlight striking down through the
trees shone around him. Judas was shivering in the frosty night;
for an instant he wondered how Jesus could endure the cold.
Judas breathed softly; he had not been heard! Then, so gently
that Judas was not even startled, a voice sounded. Jesus was
praying.

"Heavenly Father, I have proclaimed thy gospel to the disciples whom thou hast given me. They have believed thy word.
They know that my message comes from thee; they believe that
thou didst send me.

"Bless them, Heavenly Father. I am going to leave them; they
must stay in the world. Keep them by thy power, holy Father.
I have given them thy Word, and the world hates them because
they belong to thee. I do not ask thee to take them out of the
world; protect them from the evil one. Consecrate them by thy
truth; thy Word is truth. As thou hast sent me into the world,
so I have sent them into the world."

Judas stood like a statue; the Master was praying for him!
Jesus had not finished.

"I do not pray only for my disciples, Heavenly Father. I pray
for all who believe in me: make them all one together! Help
them to be one as we are one—I in them and thou in me.
O Father in heaven, just and merciful, the world has not known
thee, but I have; and my followers know that I have come from
thee. Give them the love which has bound thee to me and me
to them."

The prayer ended. How terribly calm Jesus was! He was so
sure that God was right there! With an effort Judas controlled a
mad desire to flee and instead walked quietly away. But when
he was out of earshot he broke into a run. Not knowing where
he was going, he ran until his breath came in gasps. He found
himself among houses. It was Bethany, empty and bare in the

night, but here where people lived he felt secure from the terror of the Garden where Jesus was talking with God.

Dreading to go back to the Hill of Olives, Judas slumped down on a bench beside the town well. He remembered the day he had first heard Jesus preach in Jerusalem. What mysterious power had compelled him to follow this strange Rabbi? Since then he himself had often preached the gospel of the Kingdom which he had learned from Jesus.

Judas pressed his fists against his temples. Never, never could he escape this man from Nazareth! God was in him! Every memory of his life with Jesus rose up and condemned Judas for his bargain with the priests. He could never keep it! He would go back to Jesus and confess his great sin! He stood up shivering. It was the cold of the night, he told himself. He took a few faltering steps toward Gethsemane and stopped. What could he be thinking of? Was he serious about giving up his plan to put Jesus in the power of the high priest?

Judas dropped again to the bench. He had promised to help the high priest for good reasons. Jesus *was* a very dangerous man! If he should confess his bargain to Jesus now, he might be helping to overthrow the sacred religion of his nation! No! He must go through with it! Jesus must be stopped!

The moon was pale in the dawn when Judas finally forced himself to go back to the olive orchard. He could not put Jesus' prayer out of his mind. How could he ever face him? Yet Judas found courage and strength in the thought that God knew that he was doing this difficult thing for the sake of true religion. Comforted by this, he crept to the place where the men slept and lay down on the hard ground. Just the same, his heart was cold within him as he watched the dawn change the sky.

A half hour later the sun was still hidden behind the hills of Judea; gray light filled the olive grove. The disciples slept, but Judas was wide-awake. Suddenly he heard a footfall. Among the trees he saw a figure moving toward them. For an instant panic gripped him. Was someone else guiding the priests to the place where Jesus stayed? Judas shook Peter by the shoulder.

"Simon Peter! Peter!" The fisherman did not move. Judas shook him harder.

"Eh? What is it?" Peter was heavy with sleep.

"There is someone coming." Instantly Peter was awake. Judas pointed to the man, now very near them. Peter stood up, and Judas followed him. They recognized a young man whom they had seen often in the Temple.

"I am glad to find you awake," he said to Peter. "I have come to warn you of danger." Judas' heart leaped. Had this fellow seen him going into the priests' council chamber?

"I am a student in the Temple," explained the young man. "I have heard your Rabbi every day." Peter looked closely at the face of the youth. He seemed sincere. "Yesterday the priests had a meeting. They are going to stop your Rabbi!" Fear was like a heavy hand on Judas. This fellow was going to betray him to Peter!

"What do you mean?" asked Peter. The other disciples were aroused by Peter's voice. Several sat up and stared at the three men.

"I do not know just what they plan to do," continued the student. "But I know that they want to accuse him before Pilate." Relief flooded through Judas. The man did not know!

Jesus still slept soundly, but the others gathered around. "This young man says that the priests are plotting to arrest us," Peter said to them. The dawn light, dimmed by the morning mist, threw an ashy gray color over the faces of the Twelve. Peter could see that they were afraid and very suspicious of the visitor. He turned sharply to him. "Why have you come out here?"

The young man did not hesitate. "Your Rabbi knows the truth about us. We all know he is right; that is why the others hate him so!" He looked down at Jesus. "But I believe his word! God has sent him to call us back to Him!"

Judas turned away. The courage of this young man made the disciples ashamed. After a moment James said, "We thank you for coming here." The young man smiled and answered: "I must go back to the Temple. Let no harm come to your Rabbi!"

Without comment the twelve men watched him leave. The warm sunlight awakened Jesus when the mist began to drift away. He was surprised to find all the men up. A few were talking quietly; others sat alone. Judas' back was turned. Peter came over to Jesus. "A student from the Temple came here while you slept, Master. He told us that the priests are plotting against us." All but Judas were looking at Jesus. He stood up. His cloak was soiled from constant use. Small twigs and dirt clung to the coarse cloth. But tangled hair and rumpled clothes could not hide the Master's great dignity. His voice was untroubled when he answered. "Today is the Feast of the Passover. Today the lamb is killed so that the people may be saved. The Father in heaven has sent the Son of Man to be delivered up. In a little while you will see me no more; then after a short time you will see me again."

"We do not understand what you are saying, Master," said Peter.

"You will soon be full of sorrow—but the people who hate me will be glad that they have overcome me," answered Jesus. "But your sorrow will turn to joy. Right now you are full of fear—and you will be even more afraid! But do not lose heart: I will return and give you the kind of joy that no one can take away from you."

The disciples could make nothing of Jesus' words. What could he mean by saying, "I will return"? Jesus prepared to go into Jerusalem. With growing dread, the disciples realized what he intended to do. Would he pay no attention to the warnings of the young man?

As they came into the Temple, Jesus found a large crowd that had gathered early to meet him. The disciples felt like prisoners giving up all hope of freedom.

At first not a priest or Pharisee was anywhere to be seen. So eagerly did the disciples keep watch that they hardly heard what Jesus was saying. "Do not let anyone deceive you," he warned the people. "In the last days many false prophets will come in the name of God—but do not follow them! If you are my true followers, men will hate you and try to kill you. But even when you are dragged before kings and priests and put on trial, tell everyone the gospel of God! Do not worry or try to prepare ahead of time—I will give you answers that your enemies cannot escape."

"Look!" whispered Andrew. "There they come!" Judas saw a priest he had talked to the day before walking toward Jesus. But the Master paid no attention.

"In those days," he continued, "your own friends will betray you. They will put you to death. Everyone will hate you for my sake—but do not be afraid! If you are willing to give your life for me, you shall have eternal life." Like darts his words struck into Judas.

"The time will come when Jerusalem will be surrounded by enemy armies," declared Jesus. "Then she will soon be destroyed. Let everyone flee to the hills for his life, for in those days God will punish this wicked city for her sin. Every single building will be leveled to the ground!"

"Our beautiful Temple!" cried a man in the crowd. "Look at these great stones! Will all this be destroyed?"

"I tell you solemnly," declared Jesus, "the day is coming when not one stone in this Temple will be left standing!"

The priest broke in. "How do you dare say that? This is the house of God. It took the finest workmen in Israel forty-six years to build it. God will not let his Temple be destroyed!"

"You do not know how to save your Temple!" retorted Jesus. "You think it is holy because you make many sacrifices in it! But I tell you that your enemies will tear down your Temple and kill your children, all because you do not know that God has come to you!"

"What do you mean?" exclaimed the priest. "Look at the monuments we have built in memory of the prophets!"

"You decorate the tombs of the prophets and say to yourselves, 'If we had lived then, we would have treated them better!' But you kill the prophets that God sends you, just as your ancestors did!

"Your religion is like a filthy cup: bright and shiny on the outside, but dirty inside! Your Temple is beautiful, but your religion is rotten!" The priests shrank back from the sheer force of Jesus' anger.

"You are like whitewashed tombs: clean on the outside, but inside they stink with rotten bones! You put on a show of goodness—but your hearts are filled with hypocrisy and wickedness!"

The disciples were horrified. Jesus was attacking the very priests themselves! Did he realize what would happen?

"God will punish you for killing the prophets, just as he condemned your wicked fathers for their sins! You snakes! You nest of vipers! There is no way for you to escape eternal fire!"

The priests flushed crimson. The people watched them stalk into the inner court. Judas saw the hatred on their faces and knew that they would never be satisfied until they had killed Jesus. He was glad now that he had gone over to their side.

"We had better leave this place!" whispered Andrew to Peter. He looked toward the gate where the priests had gone. But Jesus was talking to the people again.

"He will never leave!" answered Peter.

Panic seized the Zealot. "Come on! We must get out of here!" He kept looking at the guards in the tower.

"What are you thinking of?" demanded Peter, turning on him. "We can't leave the Master alone!"

"I'm not going to be caught like a rat in a trap!" The Zealot looked at the high walls around them.

"I will not leave this place until the Master does," declared James firmly.

"You will never get out," warned the Zealot.

"Just the same, I'm staying," repeated James stubbornly.

All day the crowd listened eagerly to every word that Jesus spoke. Even in their despair the disciples knew that Jesus would consider the day well spent. "How I wish he would leave!" burst out John, late that afternoon. "Where will we eat the Passover meal tonight?" During a pause he asked Jesus the question.

"You and Peter go into the city," answered Jesus. "You will meet a man carrying a water jar. Follow him to his house. Tell the owner that the Rabbi says, 'Where is the room in which I am to eat the Passover with my disciples?' This man will show you a large room upstairs, with table and couches arranged for us. Prepare the Passover meal there."

The two disciples were amazed: Jesus had planned the meal ahead of time! Glad to get out of the Temple, they did as they were told. At twilight, Jesus and the others arrived. All except Jesus were completely worn out. They had given up all hope.

Who could tell what might happen before this night was over? Like men in a daze, the disciples washed their hands in basins which Peter and John had filled with water. Then they lay down on the couches around the table.

But Jesus did not immediately lie down with the others. Curiously the men watched him take off his robe and tie a towel around his waist. He began to pour water into a basin. Then Jesus carried the basin to where Andrew lay and knelt at his couch. The fisherman hardly knew what to say. Slaves and servants washed the feet of guests! Silently Jesus washed the feet of all the Twelve, coming last to Simon Peter.

"Master! You shall not do this for me!" He drew away from Jesus, who was kneeling at the foot of his couch.

"Peter, you do not understand why I am doing this—but very soon you will!"

"I will never let you wash my feet!" protested Peter.

"Unless I wash your feet," answered Jesus gravely, "you cannot share in my suffering and my glory."

Peter realized how much this act meant to Jesus. "O Master, wash my head and my hands too!"

"No," replied Jesus, drying Peter's feet with the towel, "since I have done this, you are clean all over. No more is needed." Reverence filled the disciples as they listened to his words; but not until he had put on his robe and taken his place at the table did they understand.

"Do you know why I have done this?" he asked. "You call me your Rabbi and your Master—and that is right: I am your Master. If I am willing to wash your feet, should you not serve one another? No servant is greater than his Master. You must learn this: if any man wishes to be great in the Kingdom of Heaven, he must be the slave of all men for my sake."

The disciples began to eat. The supper was simple. A piece of roast lamb in a shallow bowl was the chief dish. There was a plate of unleavened bread, a vegetable, and a bowl of sauce made of dates, raisins, and vinegar. There was nothing else except a single large cup of wine mixed with water. Each man took a piece of meat in his hand and ate it. Some first dipped it into the vinegar sauce. The men were glad for the food, but it did not drive away their discouragement. Everyone knew it could not be long until they were arrested. Amid these dark thoughts, Jesus spoke. "The hand of him who betrays me is with me on this table!"

The disciples could hardly believe their ears.

"One of us—betray you?" asked Peter. They looked at each other.

"One of you at this table will betray me, but woe to him who does this deed!" declared Jesus.

"Is it I?" asked James. He seemed to doubt even himself.

John leaned back to Jesus. "Tell us who it is, Master."

"It is not I, is it, Rabbi?" urged Judas.

Jesus turned to him. "Are you sure it is not you?" He looked accusingly at Judas. Then Jesus said sternly, "Whatever you are planning to do—do it quickly!" Judas left the room immediately.

"He must be going out to pay for the food," remarked Andrew.

"Master, I don't care what the others may do; I will stay with you!" declared Peter.

Jesus looked at him sadly: "Peter, you are going to face a terrible test, but I have asked God to help you. You must help the others."

"Master," repeated Peter, eager to convince himself that he was not afraid, "I swear that I will do anything for you. I am ready even to die for you!"

Jesus shook his head. "You have promised more than you can do. Before the cock crows at dawn you will deny three times that you ever knew me!"

When the men had finished eating the meat, Jesus picked up a piece of the unleavened bread and held it in his hands. "I have looked forward to eating this Passover meal with you before my suffering begins." He raised his eyes. "Heavenly Father, I thank thee that thou hast shown mercy and love to thy children. I thank thee that thou hast hidden these things from the wise and revealed them to babes."

Then Jesus broke the bread and gave the pieces to the disciples, saying: "Take this bread. It is my body; I am the Bread of

Life. If you believe in me, you already have eternal life. Just as I have broken this bread, my body will be broken when I suffer for you. Every time you break bread, therefore, remember what I have done for you."

The men were not sure that they understood all that Jesus meant, but they knew they were somehow sharing the life of their Master as they took the bread and ate it. Then Jesus took the large cup of wine and water in his hand. "This cup of wine stands for a promise of salvation: take it and drink the wine, every one of you. This wine is my lifeblood, which I give that you may have eternal life. Whenever you drink it, remember my promise to you." Jesus handed the cup to John, who was reclining next to him. John sipped from it and passed it on. Reverently each man drank from the cup. Jesus put it on the table and arose from his couch. The group stood and chanted together a psalm of thanksgiving:

> "I love the Lord, because he heareth
> My voice and my supplications.
> Because he hath inclined his ear unto me,
> Therefore will I call upon him as long as I live.
> The cords of death entangled me,
> And the pains of hell laid hold on me:
> I found trouble and sorrow.
> Then called I upon the name of the Lord:
> O Lord, I beseech thee, deliver my soul.
> Gracious is the Lord, and righteous;
> Yea, our God is merciful.
> The Lord saveth the simple;
> I was discouraged, and he saved me.
> Return unto thy rest, O my soul;
> For the Lord hath blessed thee greatly."

"Come! Follow me!" Abruptly Jesus walked from the room, down the stairs, and into the dark street. The moon had just risen; it hung low over the Hill of Olives, blood-red in a black sky, giving almost no light. Jesus walked swiftly toward the city gate. The disciples glanced up and down each street they crossed, alert for any sign of soldiers.

It did not take them long to reach the foot of the Hill of Olives. Jesus did not go to their usual resting place. Instead, he led the eleven men toward his place of prayer in the Garden of Gethsemane. They were panting for breath when Jesus entered a narrow gate through the stone wall that Judas had climbed over the night before.

The Garden was dark. Among the dense trees the moon could not be seen at all. During the week, the men had slept under clear skies; but now there was a damp chill that threatened a storm on the morrow. When Jesus stopped, his followers sank wearily on the ground.

"Wait here for me while I pray," said Jesus. A note of distress had crept into his voice. He turned to Peter, James, and John. "Come with me." They groped their way through the woods, their hands before them. Jesus stopped. "My soul is very sorrowful, even to death. Wait here and pray for me." The men had never known Jesus to be like this before; he was almost appealing to them for help. A short distance away Jesus knelt on the ground. The hard day, the meal, and the walk up the hill had made the fishermen drowsy, but they heard Jesus praying very earnestly. "O Father, thou canst do all things! If it be possible, spare me this suffering. Nevertheless not my will, but thine, be done." They heard his voice no more.

Peter did not know how long he had slept when he was awakened by Jesus' shaking his shoulder. "Simon Peter! Are you sleeping? Couldn't you stay awake and pray with me even one hour?" James and John roused themselves. "Stay awake, all of you. Pray that you will not fail me now when I need you most! I know you want to be my true friends—but you have not the strength!"

Hard as the three men tried, they could not stay awake. Twice more Jesus came and aroused them. The last time Peter awoke the moon was high, but was almost hidden behind a cloud. He could make out the faint outline of the figure of Jesus standing beside him. A chilly wind had sprung up and rattled the leaves. The night wind carried a warning Peter could not understand. James and John slept heavily.

"Still resting?" said Jesus. The two men stirred and looked at

Jesus, greatly ashamed. "Come! Get up! The hour has come when the Son of Man is to be betrayed into the hands of sinful men!" Through the black woods rang the sound of a sword clanging against a steel shin guard. Peter leaped to his feet. "James! John!"

Through the gnarled trees the men saw a sight that struck terror into their hearts: led by Roman soldiers, a mob carrying torches was advancing toward them. The yellow flames whipped in the wind and cast hideous twisting shadows as they came nearer the Garden.

"They must know we are here!" whispered James. "Come on! Let's get out of here!" The two fishermen fled into the darkness.

Torchlight glinted on spears and helmets. There was no sign of the other eight disciples. Peter stood rooted to the spot from which he had risen. Jesus watched calmly. Some in the noisy crowd carried clubs. The light from the flares struck through the trees and fell full on Jesus' face.

"There he is!" The cry echoed in the Garden. A wall of smoking torches and gleaming swords and shields closed around Peter and Jesus. There was no escape now.

A Roman soldier stepped forward. "Hold up that torch!" he commanded his aide. In the wavering light he peered into the faces of Peter and Jesus. Another figure stepped from the group.

"Judas!" Peter was stunned.

"Hail, Master!" said Judas. Then very deliberately, as though forcing himself, he kissed Jesus.

"Do you betray me with a kiss, Judas?" asked Jesus, sadly. The traitor could not bear the voice of the man he had once called his Master; he turned and rushed out of the circle of Jews and soldiers. Peter never saw him again.

The captain gave a sharp command, and several soldiers stepped toward Jesus. The group of men broke into angry shouts. Jesus' stern voice rang through the clamor. "Why do you come to arrest me with swords and clubs as though I were a robber? Day after day I was in the Temple teaching—you never tried to arrest me there!"

For an instant the torches ceased waving. Then the mob surged all the more angrily upon Peter and Jesus. Peter snatched his short sword from his belt and struck a wild blow. A man cried out sharply. The captain shouted a command: soldiers pushed through the rabble and seized Jesus. A burly soldier knocked Peter backward; he fell heavily and lay still.

When Peter came to his senses, he was breathing hard. He had no idea how long he had been stretched on the ground half stunned. He lifted himself on one elbow. Torches were moving down the road. The sound of the mob was faint in his ears.

For the first time Peter realized that he was alone. The Master was gone! What would he do without him? Loneliness swept over the fisherman. He leaped to his feet and dashed headlong through the trees where the soldiers had led Jesus. He tripped over a root and plunged to his knees; branches lashed his face when he arose, but in his panic he did not feel them. He burst out onto the road. In the distance the tiny lights were going out, one by one, as the procession entered the gate of Jerusalem. With a cry of helpless despair, Peter ran down the hill toward the city.

17. THE DARKEST HOUR OF ALL

As Peter ran he realized that he did not know where the Roman soldiers were taking Jesus. What if he should lose sight of them? He was gasping for breath by the time he reached the city gate.

The Temple was closed. Would they lead the Master to Pilate? In the darkness, Peter could barely make out the massive bulk of the fortress of Antonia, the Roman prison. No sound broke the silence within its walls. Peter ran a few steps and stood panting at the first street crossing. Desperately he glanced one way and the other. If only there were someone to tell him which way they had gone with Jesus! Would they go to the house of the high priest himself? Peter turned and ran toward the south side of Jerusalem, his sandals clattering on the stone paving.

At every turn in the winding street Peter peered into the darkness, hoping to see the wavering light of torches ahead of him. He did not notice a dark figure standing against the wall of a house that closed in the narrow street until he ran into him. Startled but glad to see someone, Peter asked, "Sir, have you seen soldiers and men with clubs passing this way?" The question was out before he realized his danger. What if this stranger were an enemy? He could not even see his face.

The man's answer was cautious. "Some men went by here a few minutes ago." The voice seemed familiar to Peter. "Did they have a prisoner?" he asked.

"The torches were too dim for me to see." Peter forgot to thank the stranger in his haste to overtake Jesus. He rounded the next corner, running, then stopped short. Flickering straight ahead of him were torches. Soon he was close enough behind the men who carried them to see more clearly. The yellow flames threw weird patterns on the houses: shadows of men twisted and dodged on the walls as the torchbearers swung the lights to and fro. Peter followed cautiously, coming no closer than necessary. His heart leaped when he heard a step behind him. He jerked around and saw a young priest. Fear clutched at him. He was trapped! Before he could move, the man spoke. "There they are." Peter recognized the voice. It was the person he had run into a moment before! The priest looked at him curiously and exclaimed, "You were with the Galilean, weren't you?"

A denial sprang to Peter's lips. Then he recognized the priest: it was the student who had come to the Hill of Olives that very morning! "What are they going to do?" Peter could keep back his anxiety no longer.

The young priest shook his head gravely. "I fear the worst. Look! They have stopped!" He pointed. The torches shone on a heavy wooden gate. It swung open, and the group started to enter.

"Let's follow them in," urged the priest.

"Oh, no!" protested Peter. "They will recognize me. They wouldn't let me in anyway." But the priest was already hastening ahead. Peter followed. His friend entered with the last of the group, and the gates swung shut.

A servant woman stood outside to question everyone who wanted to go into the house of the high priest. Torches fastened

to the walls on each side of the gate threw a pool of yellow light
on the street. Peter could hear many people inside; torchlight
flickered on the high walls of the palace of the high priest, rising behind the gate. Driven by curiosity, Peter came closer and
closer. The woman looked at him but said nothing. Peter hid
his face; he was glad the torches were smoky and low.

Suddenly the gate opened, and Peter saw his friend. "Let
this man in," he ordered the servant woman. There was nothing
for Peter to do but go in. As soon as he stepped into the light
the woman said loudly: "Wait a minute! Aren't you one of this
Galilean's followers?"

Peter froze with fear. "No!" he snapped, and plunged through
the gate to get away from her. Sweat stood out on his forehead.
A narrow escape!

Peter was relieved that the large courtyard of the high priest's
palace was so crowded. He shrank into a shadowed corner and
anxiously searched for Jesus. In this great house met the San-
hedrin, the great council of all the rulers of the Jews. Peter saw
the rough soldier who had knocked him down standing outside the door. Jesus must be inside! There was nothing to do but
wait.

Peter began to feel cold. Near the center of the yard several
men had built a charcoal fire. Peter was tempted to warm his
hands, but immediately gave up the idea: these very men had
seen him in the Garden! He walked back and forth in the shadows, but it did not help much: his feet were getting numb. He
wished he had never come into the courtyard. If he tried to get
out, the woman would see him.

Fifteen minutes passed. What was happening in the priest's
dark palace? Peter shivered and pulled his coat tight around
him. How good that fire would feel! At last he could stand it no
longer. Taking care to keep the firelight from shining on his
face, he went nearer.

"How long will it take to condemn him?" Peter heard one
of the men ask impatiently.

"It won't be long," answered another. He was in the uniform
of the high priest's servants.

"Too bad his disciples got away!" growled the first. "I would

like to get hold of that one that struck Malchus with his sword!"
A man came out of the palace and joined the others around the
fire.

"He's a stubborn fellow!" exclaimed the man. "He won't answer any questions!"

"What about the witnesses?" inquired a man who had not
spoken before.

The other laughed. "They tell different stories! They can't
agree on what the Galilean said!"

"Don't worry," said the high priest's servant confidently. "No
matter what happens, they won't let him get away now." The
last spark of hope in Peter died. The priests were determined
to kill Jesus. The end had come. Peter did not notice that the
man in front of him had moved so that the firelight shone directly on his face.

"Say! Weren't you with that Galilean?" Like a thunderbolt
the question struck Peter. He stiffened with terror and cursed
himself for having dared to come near the fire. "Of course not!"
he answered gruffly, and backed away. The man who had seen
him strike Malchus with his sword had not heard the question.
Peter sighed. His luck could not last much longer.

A group of people were going through the gate. Perhaps he
could slip out without being noticed. The priest who had got
him in here had disappeared. A cry went up at the door of the
palace. Guards were coming out of the priests' council room!

Suddenly Jesus stood in the doorway. Peter's throat went
dry. What had they done to his Master? His face was swollen
from many blows. It glistened wet in the firelight—they had
spit on him! Jesus stumbled as he came down the short stone
staircase. A rough fellow kicked him. "Get along there!" He
laughed coarsely. Pity flooded through Peter, then rage at the
man who had hurt Jesus.

"What is the verdict?" A man was speaking to Peter.

"The verdict?" Peter mumbled the words stupidly. Another
man answered the question.

"He is doomed to die."

Peter looked from one to the other. "Die?"

"Yes. They are going to ask Pilate to sentence him to death."

The others looked at Peter curiously. Someone grabbed him roughly by the shoulder.

"Say, you! Didn't I see you in the olive orchard?" A guard! He waved to the others. "Come over here! Here is one of the Galileans. Listen to his accent!"

Like icy water, fear swept Peter's daze away. Faces full of scorn surrounded him. Panic-stricken, Peter wrenched loose.

"In the name of God, I never even heard of this Jesus!" he swore. "What are you talking about?" Then a shrill sound caught Peter's ear. The words stopped in his throat. Outside the wall a rooster was crowing. Peter's lips were open, but no sound came from them. He was staring at the man who had accused him, but he didn't see him. The flush of anger and panic drained from his face. Jesus had heard.

With terrible dread, Peter watched his Master turn. Their eyes met. Time stood still. Peter forgot everyone else: there were just the two of them, Master and cursing disciple. The sadness in Jesus' eyes burned through Peter. "Do you betray me too, Peter?" the Master seemed to say.

"Come on! Get going!" A guard slapped Jesus heavily. Driven by the rough men, Jesus went out of the gate.

Like a sleepwalker, Peter followed. The guards did not try to stop him. The servant woman at the gate did not notice him. For an instant he stood in the street watching the men take Jesus away. The gate closed behind him. Then the terrible dream broke; scalding tears flooded Peter's eyes. They came from his very heart. He walked a little way down the dark street and stopped, leaning against a stone wall. Desperately he pressed his face into his hands. How could he stand this bitter remorse? If only he had been faithful to his Master!

Peter was certain that the end had come; he dreaded seeing his Master condemned to death by the Roman governor, Pilate. All night he walked the deserted streets of Jerusalem. But when morning came he could not stay away from the fortress of Antonia, where he knew that Jesus would soon be brought before Pilate.

In the cold dawn it was a forbidding sight. Herod the Great, who had ruled before Pilate's time, had covered the massive rock on which the fortress stood with stones too steep and smooth for attackers to climb. The walls rose sixty feet above this and towers were built at each corner. The guards on the highest towers were one hundred and eighty feet above the pavement inside the fortress. From it they could see everything in the Temple below as well as the countryside north, east, and west of Jerusalem.

A short stairway led from the Temple porch into the fort. A crowd of men were gathered in the Temple courtyard, among them not one who had ever heard Jesus teach. Peter had lost all fear of being seen. As he waited, his mind was entirely taken up with thoughts of what might be happening to his Master behind the closed doors of Pilate's judgment hall.

Peter was surprised to see Pilate come out of the fort down the steps into the Temple. Where was Jesus? Why did Pilate come here? Then Peter remembered: the priests would not enter the Roman building, for fear of making themselves impure for the Passover.

After a delay Pilate came slowly out of the high priest's council chamber. He stopped and looked at the men crowded before him. A few cried out, "Where is the Galilean?"

Pilate waved his hand for silence. "I have examined this Jesus. He has not committed any crime."

A priest in the crowd cried out loudly: "He is stirring up the people! He has made trouble both in Galilee and in Judea."

"I have examined him, and so has Herod," declared Pilate. "We agree that he does not deserve to die. I am going to order my soldiers to whip him and let him go." The crowd was still. Then a priest cried out: "No! Away with him! He is destroying our holy religion!" The rabble in the court burst out with angry shouts: "To the cross with him!"

Pilate turned around and went into the fortress. The priests were worried lest Jesus be set free. They began to argue with the men in the courtyard. "Do not let him escape now!" they urged. "Make Pilate crucify him!" A shout arose when a group of Roman soldiers came out of the fort into the Temple; Jesus was with them.

A cry broke from Peter's lips when he saw his Master before

the crowd. Thorn branches had been twisted into a wreath and pressed on his head. He wore a purple robe. Peter could see he was in pain. "Behold! Here is the man!" cried Pilate.

"Crucify him! Crucify him!"

Pilate hesitated. "If you let him go, you are an enemy of the Roman emperor!" shouted a priest. Peter could tell that Pilate was afraid. He walked to the stone seat where he announced his decisions. Embedded in the pavement before him was the Roman seal and some Latin words. The Roman guards led Jesus to another seat. He was very weak from his beating. While the people were shouting, Pilate turned toward the priests gathered in a knot near his judgment seat and said bitterly: "You have wanted a Jewish king—well, here he is! Behold the king of the Jews!"

The high priest looked coldly at Pilate and said, "We have only one king: Caesar." Pilate looked down at the ground. There was one more possibility. This innocent Galilean might yet go free. Pilate remembered that custom allowed him to set free one prisoner at Passover time—a prisoner whom the people chose. Amid the commotion in the courtyard, Pilate stared at the Latin words on the pavement before him. If only the people would ask that Jesus be released!

"I shall let one prisoner go free," cried the governor. "Shall it be Bar-Abbas or the king of the Jews?"

A priest called out, "Give us Bar-Abbas!" Then the crowd took up the cry, "We want Bar-Abbas!"

Bar-Abbas! A murderer? Peter could hardly believe it! The cries grew louder. "Give us Bar-Abbas!"

"What shall I do with Jesus, called 'the Christ'?" Pilate asked, cornered. The people saw that he feared them, and their hateful screams made Peter shiver.

"Crucify him! Crucify him!" The crowd surged toward Jesus, and the Roman guards drew their swords to protect their prisoner. Pilate saw that only blood would satisfy the people. Amid the tumult he sat silent, his eyes once again on the Latin words before him. At last he stood up. He was beaten. The crowd was almost out of control. Several times he raised his hand and started to speak, but each time he could scarcely hear his own voice. The leader of the palace guard glanced anxiously at Pilate and waved to a group of soldiers waiting inside the fort. They made a tight circle around Jesus.

Pilate dropped his hand limply and turned to the priest. "Do with him whatever you want." The bloodthirsty mob surged toward the guards, but could not break through the line of soldiers, which stood like a steel wall until the door of the fort had slammed shut behind Jesus.

Peter made no attempt to follow. He took little notice of the men around him, who gave him curious stares. Peter walked to the place where Jesus had stood. He looked down and read the words which were written on the pavement in front of the judgment seat:

JUSTICE AND MERCY.

Pilate too had betrayed the Christ!

18. THE ROCK OF FAITH

THE Passover Feast was ended, and the pilgrims from Galilee were leaving Jerusalem. The friends of Jesus, and especially the eleven disciples, were dazed by the death of their Master. In the blackest discouragement, wondering what they should do, they gathered at the house where Jesus had eaten his last meal. They repeated over and over again the story of the things that had happened. Some talked about returning to Galilee. Two followers who lived in Emmaus, a town several miles west of Jerusalem, decided to go back to their homes.

The two men took the road that led over the hill of Calvary where Jesus had died. The cross still stood. Moving in the breeze was the sign which Pilate had ordered tacked to the very top: THE KING OF THE JEWS. At the hour of Jesus' death this hill had trembled as a storm thundered through the sky. But now Calvary was quiet. In the bright morning the two men could hardly believe that here they had heard the death cry of their Master: "My God, why hast thou forsaken me?"

When the men came near the cross, they stood silent for many minutes. Finally Cleopas, the older of the two remarked, "They haven't taken the sign down yet."

"Do you think others will be crucified on his cross, Cleopas?" asked the other.

"Perhaps." After a long silence, Cleopas added: "Do you remember the centurion who was in charge of the soldiers? Just after Jesus died, I heard him say, 'This man truly was a son of God!'"

"Do you think any of the others believed?" mused the other man.

"Most of them scoffed!" answered Cleopas bitterly. "One priest said over and over, 'You saved others—now save yourself!' and laughed." Tears of anger sprang into Cleopas' eyes.

"That is where his mother stood when he told John to take care of her," remarked his companion. At that moment the wind tore loose the parchment nailed at the top of the cross. It drifted to the ground a few yards away. The younger man looked at Cleopas: "Shall I get it?"

After a moment Cleopas replied: "No. Let it lie there. Why keep things that make us remember these days?" He turned his back on the cross and started down the hill toward Emmaus. His companion said nothing; he knew the bitterness that made Cleopas speak this way.

The road down to Emmaus was rough but heavily traveled. From all Judea, camel caravans carried olive oil and wool to Joppa, the main seaport of southern Palestine. Up from the sea rode Roman soldiers to guard Jerusalem, Jericho, and the forts across the Jordan.

Toward sunset the two travelers came in sight of the Valley of Aijalon, sloping down to the sea. Here King Saul had fought many bloody battles with the ancient Philistines. The low-hanging sun made a great golden blaze on the Mediterranean Sea, twenty miles away.

"We are not far from Emmaus now," remarked Cleopas. A warning cry sounded behind them: "Caravan!" The two men moved to the side of the road, and found, when they turned, that another traveler had joined them. He had been very close behind, but the two men had been so deep in conversation that they had not noticed him. After the camels had passed, kicking up the dust with their wide, padded feet, the stranger walked on with them.

"What is all this you are talking about?" he asked in a friendly way.

Cleopas glanced at his companion. Was it dangerous to answer frankly? Certainly they were safe here! "You must not have stayed in Jerusalem very long if you have not heard about what happened," he replied.

"What is that?" asked the man.

"It is about Jesus of Nazareth," answered Cleopas. "He was a Galilean. The common people all thought he was a Prophet. God truly had given him a message for us! He warned us to repent and give our lives to God if we wish to have eternal life." Cleopas paused and his companion took up the story.

"You see, the high priests hated Jesus because he called them hypocrites to their faces. He was right: they are cruel to the poor! They make many sacrifices, but just the same they do not really love God. Three days ago the priests took him prisoner and handed him over to Pilate to be crucified. We hoped that he would begin a great new day for our people—but now he is dead." The men had reached the foot of the hill. Green grass grew where a tiny brook trickled beside the road.

"We did have a surprise though," added Cleopas. "Some women in our group went out to the tomb where we laid him but they could not find his body! They saw a vision of angels who told them he was alive. Some of us went and looked for ourselves. His body was gone—but no one saw Jesus."

The stranger looked keenly at the two travelers. "You have read the Prophets, haven't you?" he asked. "They say that the Messiah must suffer before he can be victorious."

Cleopas looked at the man curiously. "What do you mean?" he asked.

"All the things happened just as the Prophets said," repeated the stranger. "The books of Moses say: 'The Lord thy God will raise up a Prophet among you, from among your very brethren, like me. You must listen to his word!' Is not your Rabbi that

One? And Isaiah too. He said: 'Behold, my Servant, whom I have chosen! I will put my Spirit upon him and he shall declare judgment to gentiles. He shall not strive or cry out; no one shall hear his voice in the streets!' Your master is this Servant of God! Did he not die on a cross? Isaiah said that he would be treated like a criminal!"

"But if he was the Messiah, why did the priests hate him?" cried Cleopas.

"They always kill the messengers of God. Isaiah said, 'They hear, but do not understand; they see, but their minds are blind —their hearts are cold.' These priests will not let God give them eternal life!"

All the rest of the way to Emmaus the two friends talked earnestly with this stranger who understood the Scriptures so well. They had never realized that the Prophets taught that the Messiah would die. They had always thought he would triumph over everybody! They remembered now that Jesus had said some of these very things.

At last they came to the village. It was dusk. Cleopas stopped in front of a small house. "Come in with us and spend the night, for the day is almost over," he said. With a smile, the stranger accepted.

It had been a long journey, and the three men were very hungry. After washing, Cleopas brought bread and fish to the table. They lay down on the hard couches. The guest picked up a small loaf and raised his eyes to bless it. He broke the bread and handed it to the men. They took it from him—and suddenly they knew who he was. There was only one who had ever given them bread like that! It must be the Master himself! They dropped to their knees. Joy, reverence, and fear filled them. When they looked up, Jesus was gone. "No wonder our hearts burned within us while he talked to us on the road!" exclaimed Cleopas.

"We must tell the others!" answered his companion. "Let us hurry back to Jerusalem."

By the time the moon rose, Cleopas and his companion were halfway to Jerusalem. It made the shadowed ravines between the mountains seem blacker than ever, but they were grateful for the faint light on the road. They knew that robbers could very easily hide among the rocks that lay along the highway. Yet fear was almost forgotten in their great eagerness to get to Jerusalem and tell the news: the Master was alive!

The two travelers pressed forward at a pace swifter than they would have thought possible on this steep road. For lack of breath, they talked very little. Twenty miles was a full day's journey—but it was just midnight when the two men hastened past the guards at the Joppa Gate of Jerusalem and half ran to the house where they had left their friends that morning.

The building was completely dark. Not a trace of light showed through the closed shutters. Cleopas knocked sharply on the wooden door. In the silence they heard only their own heavy breathing and realized that they were very tired. Cleopas knocked again. There was a muffled footstep inside; then the bolt scraped and the door opened a crack.

"Open up!" whispered Cleopas impatiently. It seemed to take a long time for the man at the door to recognize them and open the door. Cleopas and his friend rushed up the stairs and burst into the upper room.

Everyone was there. In the instant before he spoke, Cleopas realized that something had changed since he had left in the morning. The men were not dejected; they were talking excitedly. But Cleopas did not stop to find out why.

"We have seen him! He is alive!" The disciples leaped to their feet. James stared as though he had not understood. "We saw him on the road to Emmaus!"

"You too!" exclaimed Peter.

"He ate with us in my home," declared Cleopas. He turned to Peter in amazement. "Did you say you have seen him?"

"I saw him this morning. After the women told us they had seen a vision at the tomb, John and I went to look for ourselves. They were right! The Master's body was gone. I came back here and then set out alone for Galilee. I had traveled about an hour when the Master appeared to me, standing in the road. He commanded me to return here."

"When we first saw him, we did not know who he was," said Cleopas. Then he told everything that had happened. At first many wondered if the story could be true, but as they listened, their joy and amazement grew. When Cleopas finished, they stirred and sighed. Here was one at least who certainly believed Jesus was alive!

The air was heavy in the crowded room. An iron pan filled with burning charcoal stood near the wall. Several broiled fish, left over from supper, lay on the coals. Cleopas and his friend looked at them hungrily. Peter handed pieces to them. James rose from the rough wooden bench on which he sat and opened the shutters. Andrew poured oil from a large jar into the nearly empty lamps. The men breathed deeply of the cool air that swept through the window. The lamplight sprang up. Hope and wonder flickered through the disciples' minds, still dulled by the sorrow of the Master's violent death.

"If I could just see him myself!" murmured John.

Suddenly Jesus was there. He did not come in—he just appeared standing in the midst of them. John drew in his breath sharply. Was this a ghost? Did the others see? The men shrank from the place where Jesus stood.

"Do not be afraid. It is I! Look at my hands and my feet. Do you not see the wounds of the cross?" The men stared. In the palms of his hands James could see the marks of nails. His voice was real too! The men did not trust their eyes. Several reached out timidly and touched the scars. They moved like men in a dream.

"Have you any food?" asked Jesus. Peter took another piece of fish from the charcoal stove and handed it to Jesus. When the disciples saw their Master eat, their doubts vanished. They began to talk, trying to realize that the impossible had really happened; their Leader was really living!

"Master," burst out James enthusiastically, "are you going to drive out the Romans now and give the Kingdom back to us?" The others suddenly became quiet, listening for his answer.

"It is not for you to know when the Father in heaven will do that, James," replied Jesus. "In his own time he will destroy all evil. He has already come among you: all you must do is accept the power he gives you to obey his commands."

"Master, what do you want us to do?" asked Peter. Hearing

his brother's strong voice, Andrew could hardly believe that only that morning Peter had tried to leave Jerusalem because everything reminded him that he had denied his Lord.

Jesus looked around at the circle of his disciples and raised his hands over them. "Just as the Father sent me into the world," he said, "I am sending you. May the Holy Spirit fill you with power. Go into every part of the world and tell all men that the Christ has suffered and risen from the dead to give them eternal life. Those who repent and believe this gospel shall be forgiven their sins. But if anyone does not believe your words, the anger of God hangs over him!"

As mysteriously as he had come, Jesus left the men. They remained silent. Each man saw in the face of the others a joy none could express. At last Peter spoke: "We must let everyone know that Jesus has risen from the dead!"

Day by day the disciples learned that Jesus was doing greater things among them than he had ever done before. Faith which had been uncertain was now sure. Every afternoon the disciples went to the Temple to pray and tell the story of Jesus' power. Some people were surprised, for they thought the work of Jesus would stop when he was crucified. But many believed the word of the disciples and became followers with them.

It was not long before the success of Peter and the others came to the attention of the high priest. One day, immediately after the hour of prayer, he called his councilors together. "Did you see that fisherman who used to follow the Galilean we killed?" he demanded. "He was standing boldly in the Temple declaring that his Rabbi is alive!" Purple veins stood out on the face and throat of the angry man. "Have you ever heard such an insolent lie? They have invented the whole story from beginning to end!"

"The other men were with him," added a councilor. "They succeeded in getting the people very much stirred up."

"It must be stopped! If we can silence them with threats—all right. If not . . ." He lapsed into silence. Then his anger boiled to the surface again. "What man in his right mind could believe such a fairy tale? That upstart from Galilee—risen from the dead!"

A young priest sighed and spoke. "What can we do? Those men seem to believe very sincerely that it happened."

The high priest was instantly suspicious. "You sound as though you agreed with them," he observed bitingly. "I'll tell you what we must do! Keep a sharp watch on them. The minute they make trouble—arrest them! We can do whatever we want then."

Just before the hour of prayer the following afternoon, Peter and John entered the Temple with the worshipers who were streaming from the city. To the two disciples it seemed a long time since Jesus had been there, but nothing was changed. The row of slender columns which enclosed the inner court was majestic in the afternoon sunlight. Words of Moses, carved in the stone of the Beautiful Gate, invited every Jew to enter for prayer. There were no money-changers there. Since Jesus had driven them out, neither they nor the sellers of animals had tried to come back.

Two men carrying a cripple on a litter passed Peter and John. The disciples had seen him before, begging money from all who walked by. His helpers placed him near the Beautiful Gate as Peter and John climbed up the steps toward him. The beggar looked at them, smiled, and held out his hand. "Will you give a little money to a lame man?" he asked.

Peter and John stopped in front of the man. He was a miserable sight—dirty, ragged, and thin from hunger. His bony legs were paralyzed and useless.

"Look at us!" commanded Peter. The beggar looked at them expectantly. "We do not have any money," said Peter, "but we will give you what we do have! By the power of Jesus Christ the Nazarene, stand up and walk!" Peter stooped and pulled the man to his feet.

People had turned at the sound of Peter's voice. The beggar was standing alone! The man looked at his feet; then, utterly amazed, took a cautious step. The trumpet sounded from the roof of the Temple, calling the people to prayer, but none paid any attention; they rushed toward the beggar to see what had happened. Swiftly Peter led the man toward the outer part of the Temple courtyard. The people crowded after Peter.

At the trumpet signal the high priest left the council chamber and entered the rear gate of the inner court. How strange! The Temple was deserted! Two other priests came into the court. "What has happened?" they asked, baffled. "Where are the people?"

Through the columns, the high priest saw people running. "Look!" he exclaimed. He turned and waved to several burly guards in the uniform of the high priest's palace. "We need you here!" They followed the priests toward the sound of the crowd.

People were pushing forward to catch a glimpse of the beggar clinging to the two disciples. Peter raised his hands and cried out so all could hear: "Men of Israel, why are you so surprised at this? Why are you staring at us as though we had healed this man by our own strength? We did not do it at all!" Astonished at his words, the people became very quiet. Peter saw the high priest, but his voice did not waver.

"My friends, this man was not healed by any power of ours. He was healed in the name of Jesus of Nazareth, God's Chosen Servant. The God of Israel sent him to tell you the gospel of life, but you refused to listen to him. You handed him over to Pilate to be killed! Even when the governor wanted to release him, you demanded that this holy and just One from God should be crucified!" The high priest turned and spoke to the guards, but Peter did not hesitate a moment.

"We declare to you that God raised Jesus from the dead— we have seen him ourselves! His power healed this man! I know that you killed the Lord of Life without realizing what you were doing. But the Prophets knew this would happen to the Christ; they said he would suffer! God has chosen this way of saving you!" There was a disturbance at the edge of the crowd. Guards were thrusting the people roughly aside in their haste to get to him. "Repent now!" cried Peter boldly. "Ask God to forgive you for the terrible thing you have done, in order that your sin may be blotted out. God sent Jesus to be your Saviour!"

The guards burst through the crowd and seized Peter. Quickly his wrists were tied with rope. A cry of protest rose. Two men stepped in front of the guards as they shoved Peter toward the gate of the Roman fort next to the Temple, but they were quickly beaten off by curses and the threat of the clubs.

"What must we do?" cried a man in the crowd, cut to the heart by Peter's words.

In spite of the guards Peter bravely called out: "Repent and give your whole life to God! Believe in the name of Jesus Christ, the Saviour!"

"Silence!" The chief guard struck Peter with his club. When they came to the priests, the guards stopped. The high priest and the fisherman from Galilee stood face to face. Peter's clothes were torn, and his hands were bound behind him. The anger of the high priest had turned to scornful triumph. For a moment he stood sneering at Peter; then he stepped toward him and slapped him heavily across the face. "You liar! You will find out that you can't blaspheme the Law of God!"

Peter's face showed red marks. His eyes shone with a strange joy, and he smiled. His voice was fearless, its sound filled the whole Temple. "I shall never stop telling what I have seen with my own eyes! I shall obey God, and not man!" Pain shot through his shoulder as a guard struck him a heavy blow and shoved him roughly toward the fortress gate. Without looking back, Peter walked courageously into the Roman prison.

SCRIPTURE REFERENCES

SCRIPTURE REFERENCES

PAGES   CHAPTER 1

11.........Matt. 3:1–6
12.........Luke 3:10–16
12.........Matt. 3:7–10
13.........Matt. 3:13

CHAPTER 2

21, 22.....Luke 10:25
22.........Luke 17:20, 21
22.........Matt. 5:38–48
23.........Matt. 13:31–33
23.........Luke 5:4–11

CHAPTER 3

32.........Mark 1:23–27

CHAPTER 4

35.........Matt. 11:28
37–39.....Mark 10:17–31
40.........Luke 18:9–14
41–43.....Luke 4:16–30

CHAPTER 5

46, 47.....Luke 13:10–17
49.........Matt. 10:34
49.........Mark 6:17
50.........John 3:30
51, 52.....Mark 2:1–12

CHAPTER 6

55.........Matt. 7:1–5
57, 58.....Luke 7:36
57.........Mark 2:17
57.........Luke 5:32
60.........Mark 2:18–22
60.........Matt. 11:16–19
60.........Matt. 23:23, 24
61.........Mark 2:23–28
62, 63.....Mark 3:1–6

PAGES   CHAPTER 7

65–67.....Matt. 10:1–23
67.........Mark 3:21
68.........Mark 3:22–27
69.........Matt. 12:24–32
69.........Luke 11:27, 28
70.........Mark 3:31–35
71.........Luke 11:5–10
71, 72.....Luke 18:1–8
72.........Matt. 6:9–15
72.........Matt. 18:21, 22

CHAPTER 8

74, 75.....Matt. 11:2–15
77–79.....Mark 5:21–43

CHAPTER 9

81.........Mark 6:14–16
82, 83.....Mark 4:13–20
84, 85.....Mark 6:34
84, 85.....John 6:1–15
86, 87.....Mark 6:45–52

CHAPTER 10

92.........Mark 7:1–23
92, 93.....Mark 12:38–40
93.........Matt. 15:14
95.........John 14:1
95.........John 3:17–19
96, 97.....Mark 8:14–21
98.........Matt. 15:21–28
100, 101....Mark 8:27–30
100, 101....John 6:66–68

CHAPTER 11

102.......Matt. 16:17–20
103.......Mark 8:31–38
104, 105....Luke 4:1–13
107.......Matt. 16:25
109–112....Mark 9:14–29

PAGES   CHAPTER 12

113, 114.... Mark 9:2–10
115–119.... Mark 9:33–37
120, 121.... Mark 9:38–41
121........ Mark 9:31, 32

CHAPTER 13

126........ Luke 13:31–33
127........ Luke 10:1–12
128........ Luke 9:57, 58
128........ Luke 10:17–21
129........ Luke 9:51–56
129........ Luke 10:13–15

CHAPTER 14

133, 134.... Luke 17:11–19
136........ Mark 10:46–52
137........ Luke 19:1–10
139, 140.... Mark 11:1–11

CHAPTER 15

142........ Luke 13:6–9
145........ Mark 11:15–17
145........ John 2:13–16
147, 148.... Mark 11:27–33
148........ Mark 12:1–9
149........ Mark 12:13–17
149........ Mark 12:28–34
150, 151.... Luke 22:3–6

PAGES   CHAPTER 16

156, 157.... Mark 13:1, 2, 9–23
157, 158.... Matt. 23:25–36
158........ Mark 14:12–16
159........ John 13:1–17
160........ Mark 14:17–21
160........ Matt. 26:31–35
160........ Matt. 11:25
160, 161.... Matt. 26:26–29
162........ Mark 14:32–42
163........ Mark 14:43–50

CHAPTER 17

167–169.... Mark 14:53–72
169........ Luke 22:61
170........ Luke 23:13–16
171........ Luke 23:18–25
171........ John 18:38 to 19:16

CHAPTER 18

173–176.... Luke 24:13–35
178........ Luke 24:36–43
178........ Acts 1:6
179........ Matt. 28:18–20
179........ Luke 24:46–48
180–182.... Acts 3:1 to 4:4

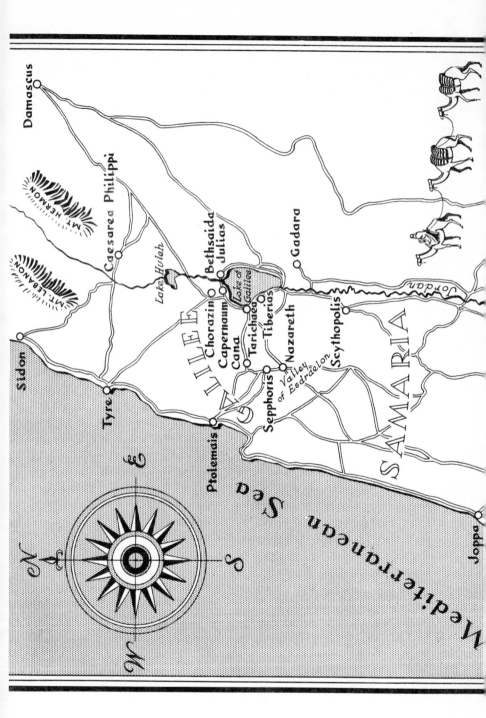

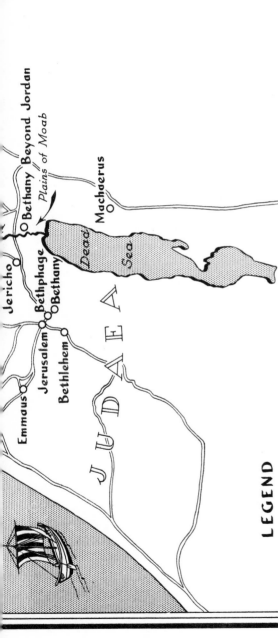

PALESTINE
In the time of Christ

SCALE OF MILES

0 5 10 15 20 25 30 35 40

LEGEND

ROADS

CITIES AND TOWNS

DISTANCES

CAPERNAUM TO NAZARETH   22 MILES
CAPERNAUM TO SIDON   55 MILES
CAPERNAUM TO JERUSALEM   90 MILES
JERUSALEM TO JERICHO   14 MILES
JERUSALEM TO EMMAUS   15 MILES

Bethany Beyond Jordan

Plains of Moab

Machaerus

Jericho

Bethphage

Bethany

Dead Sea

Jerusalem

Bethlehem

Emmaus

J U D A E A